To Deborah.

Enjoy the read!

Soar Despite Your Dodo Sales Manager

Written by
Lee B. Salz

W Business
Books

an imprint of New Win Publishing
a division of Academic Learning Company, LLC

Library of Congress Cataloging-in-Publication Data

Salz, Lee B.
  Soar despite your dodo sales manager / Lee B. Salz.
    p. cm.
  Includes bibliographical references and index.
  ISBN 978-0-8329-5009-4
  1. Selling. I. Title.
HF5438.25.S2595 2007
658.85–dc22
                          2007012852

Dedications

To my wife, Sharon, always remember,
"If you can dream it, you can have it."

To my children, Jamie, Steven, and David,
"Believe in yourself and you can accomplish anything."

To the salespeople that took the leap of faith and
felt comfortable, feeling uncomfortable,
thank you for entrusting me.

Contents

Foreword

Congratulations! You have taken an important first step in improving your sales game. But buying this book is only the first step. I know many of you may not go any further than reading this book. That would be a true shame. In the last fourteen years, I've trained over 14,000 salespeople in multiple industries. What I discovered is that so many of them think they have mastered the game of sales. They think they know it all. Well, I'm here to tell you that they don't. Sales is a philosophy, and therefore you never know everything. That's why reading this book is so critical.

Quite frankly, this book is going to change your sales career and help you drive past the competition! What makes me so certain? In addition to the 14,000 salespeople whom I've trained, I've worked with over 2,000 sales executives. Of all of them, Lee Salz is the best I've seen at building and developing sales organizations. Can I let you in on a dirty little secret? The state of sales management today is in bad shape and it's not the managers' fault...yet you suffer the consequences. There has been a twenty five-year gap in front-line sales management development. Unfortunately, you pay the price for a manager who is ill-equipped to recognize and develop your full potential.

You see, a real sales manager is supposed to be your coach. Just like a professional sports coach, he should challenge you, teach you, train you, and mentor you on an ongoing basis. In the same way, your sales manager is supposed to help develop your game and make you stronger, faster, and better – and Lee actually does that. That is why his salespeople are at the top of their game. Unfortunately, you probably aren't experiencing this – which is why you picked up this book in the first place. The good news is that Lee can help you to be successful where your manager cannot.

Why am I telling you all of this? Because if you want to be the best in your industry, the responsibility falls on you to learn all you can... and Lee is here to be your personal sales coach. Do you know the expression "you don't know what you don't know"? Well, if you are under the age of forty-two, odds are that you fit into that category. See, there was a time when Fortune 500 companies sent you through eighteen months of professional sales training and four to six weeks of additional training each year after that. Sadly, that went away with downsizing in the 80's (when some of you probably weren't even working yet!).

Even if you had the opportunity to go through that training, what are you doing today to improve yourself? Doctors, lawyers, accountants, and other professionals are required to complete continuing education courses every year in order to maintain their certification. How many of you would still be certified if the sales profession adopted that standard? Even professional athletes are required to continuously hone their skills!

Quite frankly, I have seen Lee crack the sales code over and over again at multiple companies in multiple industries. He is a master at coaching salespeople to achieve extraordinary results...because he has a formula that works! I've read hundreds of sales books and what makes this book different from all the others is that it is written from the point of view of someone who has done what he says. This isn't conceptual stuff that has never been done, or a high-level plan with no details. You won't find yourself getting frustrated by concepts that are difficult to understand. Instead, Lee offers a practical plan that you can easily implement. He presents a methodology that you can benefit from today!

Not only have I seen the results of his success, but I have had the opportunity to work with his sales teams. All of them talk about his Sales Architecture® methodology and the benefits of his program. They talk about success levels and earnings that they never had before. What makes Lee so good? He has the rare ability to see both the forest and the trees. He can formulate the overall strategy and also provide all of the steps necessary to implement it. His knowledge and wisdom are grounded in reality because he has worked side-by-side with his teams in the trenches for over fifteen years – unlike the traditional sales trainer who hasn't sold for years and is entrenched in a one-size-fits-all sales methodology, or some academic who understands the theory and writes book after book, but lacks hands-on experience.

For many years, one of Lee's goals was to share his success formula with other salespeople who were looking to be the best in their industry. He has now done that. *Soar Despite Your Dodo Sales Manager* is the culmination of Lee's experience with his sales teams and is a true gift to the sales world.

Read, implement, tell your friends, and enjoy the gift. Master this material and it will transform your sales career!

Andy Miller

President

Sales Management Guru

SMguru.com

CHAPTER 1
Hey! What's Going on Here?

*"Only those who will risk going too far can possibly
find out how far one can go."*
—T.S. Eliot

The New Job

It's a beautiful day. You wake up ready to conquer the world. And why not? It's your first day selling for your new company. You pick out your best shirt and slacks. You look in the mirror and psych yourself up about this new opportunity.

"I'm going to make a mint at this place!" But there is also a little voice in the back of your head that has doubts. After all, you had a pretty good job before this one. Things were going well in the last place, but the thought of selling a different product and making more money were too enticing to pass up. You quell the little voice by reassuring yourself that this is a great opportunity.

Off to work you go, of course, with a pit stop at Starbucks first. Arriving in the parking lot at 7:58 A.M., you are ready to go. You check your hair in the rearview mirror and perform the age-old breath test: breathing into your palm and attempting to determine your breath status. It's time to walk into the new office. Sitting in the lobby waiting for your new sales manager to greet you, butterflies stir in your belly. "This is going to be great, I hope." After a few moments, the sales manager, with a big smile, welcomes you to the company.

Eager to learn how to sell for this company, you've got your pen out, poised to take notes. The sales manager takes you to her office. The ink is ready to fly out of your pen! Here they come, the words of wisdom you've been waiting for.

"Let me share a few things with you about our company," she says.

First, we expect you to arrive at 8:00 A.M., and the day isn't over until you hit your daily sales goal. By the way, your goal is to sell 20 units per day. Let me show you to your phone. Here is the phone book. Good luck!

"Good luck?" How is that helpful? Granted, I'm not a new sales-person. I've sold successfully for many of years, you begin to think. But every company and industry is different. How do I apply my skills here? Which companies are best to call? What's different about this product? Who buys this stuff? What motivates them to buy it? And why from *this* company? All of these are very important questions that need to be answered in order to succeed in selling for this company.

You spend your first day dialing away. Rejection after rejection. At the end of the day, you've sold nothing. The butterflies from this morning are starting to feel like buzzards now. But tomorrow is going to be a better day.

Again, arriving at 7:58 A.M., you stop by the sales manager's office and ask some of the questions that were on your mind the day before.

"Which companies should I call first?" you ask.

"The large ones," she retorts.

"What's different about this company versus the competition?"

"We are the best," she proudly responds.

Somewhat convinced, but optimistic, you are off for day two of calling. You start calling the *large ones*. Today, you tell them you are the best at what you do. Day two ends, no sales. It feels as if those buzzards are now attacking your stomach. On the drive home, you start to have some doubts. Maybe I'll keep my options open. I'll keep searching Careerbuilder and Monster and see what else is out there.

After a few more frustrating days, you return to the manager's office.

"I've sold nothing so far," you begin.

"I know," she responds. "How come?"

"I don't know," you admit. "I've sold successfully before. You saw that on my résumé. I've been a top performer at every company for which I've worked."

"Well, you need to hit your goals," she admonishes. "You need to make yourself successful. Make today better."

"I'll do it!" you declare.

Off you go for another day in the trenches. More calls, no sales. Home you go, where your beloved asks how things are going with the new job. "Great!" you say, as you don't want to create alarm. She buys it, but you don't.

The next morning the sales manager asks to see you in her office, instead of the other way around.

"Where are your sales? You have to apply yourself. Make more calls. Push! Push! Push!" she implores.

You shuffle back to your desk hoping today will be better. It isn't. No sales.

Home you go. Do you quit? Do you wait to be fired? Only time will tell.

It's The Same Job...Isn't It?

This scenario plays out in companies every day. "I don't want to hear excuses. Where is the revenue? I hired you to hit your quota!" Ever heard this? If you have been in sales for a day, I'm sure you have.

Almost every sales manager in the profession utters this expression. It has been the mantra of sales managers since the beginning of time. The challenge salespeople have is that management wants the revenue, but does not necessarily provide the infrastructure and tools needed to achieve that goal. The overwhelming majority of sales managers do not and, quite frankly, cannot support their team's selling efforts.

For a moment, let's feel some sympathy for sales managers. After all, it isn't their fault. In most cases, these sales managers were great salespeople who got promoted. They earned the next rung on the ladder, which is what most of you probably aspire to do as well. So there isn't a problem, right? Wrong! The job of the sales manager is very different than the job of the salesperson, but most organizations do not appreciate the significance of this difference and leave this poor individual completely unprepared to *lead* a team.

> ### Selling and managing necessitate
> ### two completely different skill sets.

"Get them to do what you were doing," is the only marching order given to this poor schlep. No training, no development, nothing! Except of course, other than the supportive pat on the back received from their superiors. The expectation is that these managers will execute "disciple selling" with the thought being that this manager has been successful selling and the sales team will just replicate their approach. Thus, huge sales will transpire." Just have your salespeople copy what you were doing, and we'll grow revenue six fold." Nice try. This rarely works.

The challenge with executing the "disciple strategy" is that selling is personal. What worked for this top salesperson is not necessarily going to work for the group. Most top salespeople have their own creative style and approach that yields results for them, but it won't work for the masses because it's not a process and is not replicable. Sure, these managers can teach some tactics, or share some tools that helped them close a deal. They cannot, however, create the macro-selling environment needed for each team member to be successful, because that is a completely different skill.

It's amazing how many business executives have not figured out that sales managers and salespeople perform vastly different jobs. They claim to understand the difference, but their actions show evidence to the contrary. Excellence in one position is not necessarily a guarantor of success in the other. For the most part, the sports world has figured this out. The best managers are not necessarily the best players. Don't believe it? Just look at one of my favorite examples of this: Charley Lau.

In the 1980s, no other hitting coach was more recognized for his expertise than Charley Lau. His most famous protégé was George Brett who, under Lau's guidance, almost reached the rare milestone of hitting .400 (he finished the season at .390). This was at a time when only about 1.5 percent of all players reached .300. George Brett is just one of the many baseball stars that Lau molded into a terrific hitter[1].

None of this would have happened if Charley's player statistics were used in determining whether or not to hire him as a hitting coach. Why? Charely Lau was a mediocre hitter. Truth be told, "mediocre" is actually a compliment. Over 11 seasons, Lau only achieved a .255 batting average, which would not lead one to believe he would become a hitting guru. That said, this is not an endorsement for hiring mediocre talent for sales or sales management positions. It is a reminder, however, that different jobs require different skill sets.

Salespeople are hired for various roles such as prospecting, developing, and growing accounts. Sales management needs to create an environment that helps the salespeople identify where to

---

[1]Information from http://sports.espn.go.com/mlbhist/alltime/playercard?playerId=7813&type=0

prospect and how to prospect in their particular company. It is expected that sales management will help the salespeople to grow and succeed. But if no one trained them how to do it, how can anyone expect that of them? So it is left to you, the salesperson, to fill the void or fail. Sorry to be so blunt, but that's just the way it is.

Another example of the skill difference between player and manager is Tony LaRussa who has won over 2,000 games as a baseball-team manager. Look for his statistics as a major-league baseball player, and there is nothing worth mentioning. However, he has been a successful manager for the Chicago White Sox, Oakland Athletics, and St. Louis Cardinals. As a player, he only accomplished a .199 career batting average which is subpar, to say the least. Would you think that Tony was a superstar manager in the making? Remember, he doesn't need to hit a baseball as a manager. However, he does need to identify the best nine people to place upon the baseball diamond each and every day. According to *majorleaguebaseball.com*, he is ranked eighth in a list of the top 10 of winningist baseball managers. He has taken the St. Louis Cardinals to the postseason each of the last few years and won the World Series in 2006. He is best known as a data guru who uses statistics as part of his success strategy.

The converse has happened as well. Many superstar baseball players have been promoted to manager with little success. Their main responsibility is not hitting the homerun or striking out a batter, it's building a cohesive group of twenty-five players focused on winning as many baseball games as possible. Top salespeople can become terrible managers. Mediocre salespeople can become fantastic managers. Different skill sets, different results.

My Gift to You

While I am sympathetic to sales managers who were either erroneously placed or poorly trained, this book is not written for them.

(The sequel to this book *will* be.) It is for you, the salesperson who was hired to generate sales, but not given the support system or tools needed to be successful. The title of this book is *not* intended to portray a negative image of sales managers nor is it meant to be a critique of them. The old expression of not knowing what you don't know rings true here.

While you may have chuckled when you read the title, it wasn't meant to be funny. This is a serious issue that has reached epidemic levels in business. Remember, dodos were not dumb, they were unable to adapt to their environment because they never learned to fly. In my mind, the converse of the dodo is the eagle that soars majestically across the sky. This beautiful bird depicts power, control, and independence. Throughout this book, you will see references to eagle salespeople which is my way of sharing with you what the best of the best do.

Your sales manager probably has good sales skills—darn-good sales skills—and is quite probably very intelligent. This is why she got hired or promoted to that position in the first place. (I will refer to the sales manager here as "she" for clarification purposes.) But, she just doesn't know how to build a sales organization nor help others become successful, which is a vastly different skill set than selling deals themselves. Selling is for the individual. Sales management is about creating a scalable selling environment for the masses. Don't kid yourself. Sales managers are not about to become extinct like the dodo. There is a tremendous need for them. Looking at successful teams, you will clearly see a pattern. Successful teams are comprised of a group of focused, motivated individuals that are well-prepared to win with a solid leader at the helm.

While I feel sympathy for the dodo sales manager, the fact remains that she is still holding you, the salesperson, accountable for achieving quota despite her inability to provide the structure and necessary tools. I'm not proposing that you contradict her directives unless you wish to be fired. Generally, she will not give any orders other than to go sell, which is obviously what you are there to do anyway. It is her responsibility to ask for results, as the company holds her accountable for achieving their goal. Few companies hold managers accountable for developing the plan to help their team achieve that goal. What is needed is a method of achieving that goal; what is needed is the development of your personal Sales Architecture®. During my years of building and managing sales teams, the importance of creating a framework that helped salespeople be successful, yet still allowed them to be creative was the most important value I brought to my teams. I was so passionate about the concept of Sales Architecture that I trademarked it years ago.

It's interesting when speaking to business owners about salespeople. Most feel they can hire the superstars and they should be successful with little contribution from the company or sales management in support of them. That couldn't be further from the truth. To contrast, I've adopted two adult dogs from animal shelters. My first dog was like a dog in a box. He was perfectly trained, knew to sit, stayed away from the dinner table, and was completely docile with no training. We came home from the shelter and somehow, he already knew the rules of the house.

Thinking that this could be easily replicated, we adopted another dog from the shelter. Well, this dog was more of what an owner should expect. She required training and development, and today is as well-behaved as my other dog. She had the ability to learn and grow, but needed training to be successful in our home. In neither case did we know the history of the dog; they had both been strays. That made it incumbent on my wife and me (really, my wife gets the credit here) to develop them.

The same can be said about salespeople. It is rare to find a salesperson that is a *salesperson in a box* who needs no development or structure to be successful. If that were the case, there would be no need for sales management. Anecdotally speaking, 5 percent of all salespeople will be successful regardless of the support the company gives them. There is a term for these people: entrepreneurs. You don't usually find them in a sales capacity within a company; they are business owners. Another 5 percent of all salespeople will fail regardless of what is done for them. These folks probably don't belong in sales. After all, the sales profession isn't for everyone. That means that 90 percent of the sales professional pool is in the limbo group. The limbo group, as I refer to it, needs to have a firm support system in place to be successful: the aforementioned Sales Architecture.

Chances are that you fall within this group, since the large majority of salespeople exist within this category. Your sales manager is looking for results, but has probably left you without the systems needed to generate the success she wants. What do you do? You can pout beside the water cooler, which puts no dollars in your pocket. Or you can create your own structure, your own personal selling system. Sales Architecture is the framework designed to ensure your selling success. Granted, it would have been helpful if the sales manager developed this, but, as I shared before, she hasn't been taught how to develop it either. Sales managers might put some pieces together, but not the overall roadmap, which is needed to be successful.

That's where this book comes in. This work is designed to help those salespeople working for the dodo sales manager who wants results but is unable to create the necessary selling environment. For those of you now thinking that this environment is a synonym for micro-management, it most certainly is not. It is a support system leading you to success. It is a "how to" guide for selling which teaches you how to take control of your career and thus, your selling destiny. Don't be fooled! It is not Sales 101. Many of the concepts presented in this book are sophisticated and conceptual. You won't find scripts for memorization in here. As I stated before, selling is personal. How can I give you scripts if selling is personal?

It was very important to me when I wrote this book that I not write from the view of the famous "ivory tower" which is the lecture-style sales book written by CEOs that is so far from reality that it helps few of you. I also did not want to come across in an academic style. Not that I am not educated on this subject, but many books written by academics lack the real-world experience of doing it. The third key for me was to provide you with a plan you could implement. Many sales books and motivational speakers tell you to do various things, the right things, but they don't walk you through how to implement them into your process.

I've been in the trenches with salespeople for more years than I care to share, working side by side with them. We won a lot, lost some, but grew together on each adventure. My hope is that you take the concepts presented within this book in the spirit that I intended, which is as a fellow comrade. Look, I've made mistakes along the way. Why not help others avoid making those same mistakes? I've learned a few pearls as well. Why not share those too?

Where to Go From Here

This book is going to take you on a journey to help you build your own Sales Architecture. Once you know the company you are with is the best match for you, you will be able to apply the concepts in this book to help you do the following and much, much more like:

- ◆ Change your perspective from selling a prospect to facilitating a buying process.

- ◆ Develop a territory management approach so you invest your time wisely.

- ◆ Differentiate your company, your product, and yourself so buying players can understand it.

- ◆ Articulate a sound-byte, positioning your differentiated areas.

- ◆ Formulate prospecting strategies.

- ◆ Profile and analyze buying players in a unique way.

- ◆ Formulate a needs analysis program to qualify an account and differentiate yourself.

- ◆ Get deals unstuck.

- ◆ Resolve client concerns instead of overcoming objections.

With these thoughts in mind, I look forward to you soaring like an eagle with success, career satisfaction, and financial rewards firmly clasped in your talons. You will leave the dodo wondering how you became so successful.

Embrace your career and fly!

CHAPTER 2
Finding the Right Place to Hang Your Hat

"Success is not the key to happiness. Happiness is the key to success.
If you love what you are doing, you will be successful."

—Herman Cain, American businessman

Money Can Make You Do Silly Things

Money! This is the traditional answer given by salespeople when the interviewer asks what motivates them. It is also the Achilles' heel of many. Blinded by the potential earning opportunity, many join a company to sell in an environment that may not be best for them. It's easy to fall prey to this. After all, money makes the world go around. This reminds me of the old Indiana Jones movies where the treasure looked like it was ten steps away, but those ten steps were lined with dead bodies. Those flawed individuals thought they could simply grab the treasure without consideration for the perilous environment.They ran for the treasure and got shot in the process. Indiana Jones, on the other hand, was always strategic, considered what it took to get the treasure, and ultimately got it.

Employers write ads to attract salespeople to apply for positions within their company. Many overstate the earning possibilities. Truth be told, they confuse "possible" with "potential." Sure, you could potentially earn $100,000, but what does it take for someone to earn that at this company? What percentage of the salespeople actually earns this much money? This is a great question to ask.

Often, the company has one salesperson who has been with the firm since its inception and earns top dollar while the rest of the sales team has mediocre earnings.

As I mentioned, money is an easy lure, but it may not be attainable. The question to ask yourself is, are you in the right place? You have to be honest with yourself. If you aren't, you have a high risk of pursuing the wrong opportunity. I don't know where you work today, but are you sure it is the right place for you? You may have a skill set that does not match your job responsibilities. In essence, let's not force a square peg into a round hole. An individual's needs, wants, and desires may not match the employer's criteria. As you may know, many employers have job descriptions to which they compare their sales candidates. I've always recommended that salespeople do the same. There are assessments that will help provide some introspection. I emphasize this point because the concepts I share later in this book only work if you are in the best place for your skills. They have to match.

I've spoken with many salespeople and what I often hear is that many of them are mismatched to their job. For example, some are experts at cold-calling and truly love the hunt for a new client, the challenge of the chase! Others would rather work with existing clientele, leverage those relationships, and sell more products and services to them. This is the contrast between the hunter and farmer salespeople. The skill set for each of these is vastly different from one another. Hunters rarely succeed as farmers and vice versa. This is just one of the elements to consider. Later, I will share with you how to screen a career opportunity while the employer screens you. In essence, this chapter will teach you how to create your ideal selling opportunity profile in much the same way as you would define an ideal client.

While it seems logical that employers will screen out those salespeople who don't fit the profile, let's remember that they aren't experts at it either. Therefore, the responsibility lies with you, the salesperson, to control your own destiny. One way is to look at the analysis of employment in much the same way as one looks at purchasing a home. Think about all of the considerations when going through that process. How many bedrooms are needed? What is the layout of the kitchen? How many bathrooms are there? What is the quality of the school system? How far is it from work? How are the neighbors? This is just to name a few. It is a tedious process that requires interviewing the employer as much as they interview you. However, without a clearly defined profile specifying your requirements, this is not easily done. By the end of this chapter, you will be ready to create that profile.

The Story of the Rainmaker

The sales manager has a dream. She hires a salesperson requiring no training or management, and, in his first month, he closes the biggest deal in the history of the company. While dreaming this dream, the sales manager receives a résumé from someone with ten years of successful sales performance for IBM, Hewlett Packard, and Microsoft. She tells Human Resources to find a way to get this rainmaker on the payroll. Money is no object! The employer will guarantee him the world because success is imminent. No one with this pedigree could fail. How could he? The deal is made and the rainmaker is hired. Expectations are high as he goes out on his first sales call.

A month goes by with only a modicum of success. After three months, the manager starts to wonder why the company is paying this supposed rainmaker twice as much as the rest of the sales team. After six months of marginal success and a lot of paid salary (and I mean a *lot*), the company decides to let the rainmaker go. The assessment: he can't sell. He's cost the company a bundle, and worse, crushed the manager's dream.

The company feels misled and that it was the employee's fault. But what about this rainmaker who left a job with a major employer to take this risk and now is unemployed? How much responsibility did the salesperson have for this being a failure? Most of the time, the salesperson is as responsible for the turn of events as the employer. In essence, the blame is mutually shared. The exception is when erroneours expectations have been set by the employer, as in, "You will earn $100,000 in your first six months with the company." Other than that, it is usually mutual. It comes back to the importance of interviewing the company while they interview you. Sometimes, this is difficult to do, but it is critical to avoid being the tragic hero in a rainmaker movie. By the way, there is not an Academy Award given for that role.

In the case of this particular rainmaker, he failed because his skillset did not match the environment in which he was hired to sell. He was used to working for a company with a million-dollar marketing budget, making it a household name. He never had to sell the *company;* corporate did that for him. When he made an introductory phone call to a prospect and mentioned his company's name, a meeting was accepted with a sale not far behind. He benefited from the old bromide, "no one ever got fired for buying IBM." In the new company, he found a number of hurdles that needed to be overcome before that initial meeting was accepted. He also found himself selling for a company with a limited marketing budget, and low name recognition in the marketplace. To be successful, the rainmaker had to sell the company as much as the product. Maybe he hadn't considered that part of the job in his evaluation. His experience certainly had not prepared him for this challenge. In this scenario, a high level of creativity and persuasiveness was needed to position the company as credible and reputable, which was not ever needed when selling for companies like Microsoft.

Living in the Washington D.C.-Metro area during the turn of the century, I saw many of my friends leave great jobs with household name companies to pursue the dream of a dot-com income-rich life. In those new roles, these salespeople were selling for companies like ABC Technology, Inc. No name recognition. No brand recognition. Few marketing dollars. No prospects calling in. Few of these folks succeeded; few of those *companies* succeeded. These salespeople were thought to be rainmakers, but could not deliver. It wasn't because they duped the dot-com. It wasn't because they weren't great salespeople. It was because there are a number of factors that affect a salesperson's success and failure. They did not evaluate the opportunity in a way that led them to determine if they matched the company's needs and vice versa. Blinded by potential income windfall from stock options, they rolled the dice hoping that their company would go IPO.

Needless to say, those who lacked the ability to sell company credibility quickly found trouble. Why? They were mismatched to the opportunity. The requirements to be successful in their new world were vastly different than those necessary in their past world. Never before did they have to sell a company to get in the door. They had been selling IBM or Microsoft or AT&T. People knew the brand and they were involved in every buying process. To effectively position a solution, credibility had to be developed first. It was very common for these salespeople to hear from buyers, "What company are you with again? I'm not familiar with the name."

> **Earnings are very important. Make sure the suggested earnings are attainable.**

The mismatch of salespeople to the company is one of the things that prohibited dot-coms from generating the revenue they needed to survive. In addition to the bottom falling out of Wall Street stock prices, many of these companies hired the wrong sales talent to drive their business. Salespeople were all too eager to jump on a dot-com train. Few asked where the train was going and thus, got on the wrong one.

The sales manager in this scenario is not without blame. Logic would say that they would be screening for the match in the interview process. Not often is this the case. When I talk about deficiencies in sales managers' skills, evaluating talent is one of the first ones to expose itself. Sales managers have not been trained to evaluate talent, which is a skill that is learned over time with mentoring. These managers especially struggle when they are hiring someone who has worked in the industry, as they are blinded by the industry jargon. Candidates with great pedigrees also blind them.

My hope is that you recognize that you have as much to lose as they do by signing up for the wrong job. Job-hopping will ultimately hurt your résumé, and it becomes very difficult to explain in the interview process. Sales managers are looking for strong salespeople. If 100 sales managers were surveyed, 100 would say that they were looking for strong salespeople. The problem is that the term "strong" is vague. What does "strong" mean? There are a number of considerations for the profile. One qualification could be the ability to create demand for a product. In a different company, the sales need is for salespeople who are adept in selling environments in which the demand exists and the sale is based on persuading the client to buy from them versus the competition. Some refer to this as takeaway business. While both are versions of what is referred to as a hunter, each requires a different skill set to be successful.

The challenge of evaluating talent is not limited to large or small companies. It is an issue everywhere. It is costly and painful for all involved, but salespeople can avoid it by developing their ideal opportunity profile and using it to determine their match to a prospective employer.

Finding the Match Made in Heaven

The perfect match is possible to find. Maybe "perfect" is an over-statement. You can find the right match if you have taken the time to build your ideal opportunity profile. Money is not where you start, but it is an important consideration. It cannot be allowed to blind you in the evaluation process. I don't undervalue the importance of money; it is very important, but it is an unattainable mirage if your profile does not match the opportunity. When searching for sales jobs, many sales people only worry about how much money the employer is willing to pay them. Equity, stock options, 10 percent salary increase. Don't get me wrong—sales is about making money. That is why so many do it. But how long will you get to do it if you are not really what the employer had in mind? If you don't have the requisite skills, will the commissions ever be earned? How long will you stay if you aren't happy with the job?

I look at the job search in much the same way that someone looks for a spouse. Many people have a profile in their minds of their perfect mate, the things that they feel make for a perfect match. This profile may include religion, political views, interests, and even appearance. Dating becomes simply a matching game. In some respects, one could argue that it is arrogant to do this, but the counterargument is that you are simply being honest with yourself. Like the salesperson blinded by money, those who were blinded by one element, such as beauty, and forgot the others were often reminded later of the short-sightedness of their decision during an expensive divorce. It may explain why more than one in two marriages fail.

> **Being honest and thorough are the two biggest keys in determining your ideal sales opportunity profile.**

Remember, every company is looking for their rainmaker, that salesperson who will bring a huge book of business that yields results on their very first day with the organization. Don't fool yourself! This rarely happens. Most clients are not easily portable. The mistake often made is that a salesperson will paint a picture for a prospective employer that leads them to believe that they can bring a significant amount of business to the company, and the employer is all too eager to believe it. The clock begins to tick as the boss looks for the revenue. After ninety days with no revenue, the employer becomes doubtful. After all, the salesperson negotiated a great package based on this contribution. At the six-month window, the employer has forgotten about the skills and is solely focused on the feast that was going to be provided and never was. You're gone! Or worse, you get yourself sued for violating a non-compete agreement or the Uniform Trade Secrets Act. Either way, it's bad news.

Here is something worth considering: if you represent that you can move clients, you are stealing assets from your current employer. Many prospective employers think about how you will leave their employment as much as how your tenure will be while you are there. If you will attempt to take your current employer's clients, you will probably try to take theirs. This can cause a concern with the hiring manager and can eliminate you from consideration. Position this delicately, if at all.

Donning my humble hat for a moment, I recall a time where one of my competitors was struggling and their salespeople were leaving in droves. Quickly, I jumped out and hired five of their top salespeople without any consideration for a candidate profile. We had to move fast so no one else acquired this talent. Our thinking was that these folks knew the industry, and thus, they would be successful quickly. As you can probably guess, it didn't work. Within four months, we had let all of them go. What I did not mention was that these salespeople were used to selling at the low-price level. We were a boutique. Not only were we a boutique, we were a start-up with no name recognition. Their company had a tremendous brand presence in the marketplace.

Not one of them was able to make the shift. At the time, we accused them of being poor salespeople. We felt misled, tricked, and duped. In hindsight, we actually shared the blame. Had we utilized our candidate profile, we never would have hired any of them. Considering their former success profile would have helped determine the fit. On their end, they were left with a four-month stay with an employer on their résumé. We both lost.

Career Introspection

By now, you probably appreciate the importance of developing your specific opportunity profile. To do so, there are two concepts to review, traits and behaviors. You have probably heard those terms before. If you took Psychology 101 in college, you likely learned that these terms are polar opposites. Traits are the attributes of an individual that cannot change. He is who he is. In genetics, examples of traits are eye color, attached ear lobes, and hair color. These are typically thought of as genetic traits which are the result of the combination of the parents' genes. They are classified as dominant and recessive. Traits are considered unchangeable (contacts, surgery, and hairstylists aside).

For purposes of developing the profile, traits are the unchangeable aspects of you. They are your experiences in selling such as company type, product or service type, sales cycle, etc. These are unchangeable aspects. At the opposite end of the spectrum is behaviors. These are your changeable aspects, if you desire to change them. Needless to say, this can involve an enormous investment of time and energy. Are you up for that? Not everyone is. It also involves risk for both you and your employer. From the employer point of view, it is important to know:

- What do they expect of a salesperson?

- What skills are they willing to teach?

- What is their commitment to training and development?

- What won't they teach?

- What do they feel can't be taught?

It is also important to re-word those questions and ask them of yourself:

- What do you expect of an employer?

- What skills do you want to learn?

- How committed are you to learning?

- What don't you want to be taught?

Putting those two sequences together allows you to better understand the match between your needs and those of a potential employer. I'm not suggesting that you directly ask potential employers these questions, but during the interview process, this information can be gleaned. For example, if you have never cold-called, but desire to learn to, you want to understand the employer's commitment to teaching this skill. If you have sold in a transactional sale, but desire a more complex one, will the employer teach you? How will they teach you?

At the other end of the spectrum, if a manager feels that cold-calling is a required skill to be hired, and you haven't done it, you probably will not be considered even though you are willing to learn the skill. If you aren't going to win, lose early. That is why it is important to understand the expectations of sales behaviors. It's not a right-versus-wrong scenario, but a quest to understand the employer's perspective in contrast with your own requirements.

A factor often not considered by sales candidates is what they have historically sold. Those who have been selling services are typically used to an environment that allows them to customize, configure, and create based on client requirements. However, those who have historically sold products have usually been limited to the proverbial box. What the gadget does, it does. What it doesn't do, they hope the next version does. The fixed product is exactly that: fixed. It is the same every time. As a salesperson, you aren't expected to create the solution. However, in many service sales, a core requirement of the salesperson is the ability to craft the ideal service solution based on the needs of the prospect. If you haven't sold products before, is this something you want to learn? If you haven't sold services, is this something you want to learn?

The best example depicting the extreme of the product/service conundrum is in the field of information-technology development. These firms don't have a product. They don't have a defined service either. They have coders, IT developers who build to a client's specific requirement. But what requirement? Imagine selling for a firm in which you have no product, no defined service. Each time you call on a prospect, you figure out if there is something to be sold. If there is, what the heck is it? Some salespeople love that environment and thrive in it. They love the challenge of creativity. Others get frustrated very quickly and quit.

Hunters and Farmers

Another key area for review is the hunter/farmer relationship that I referenced before. In the graph, I have contrasted these in what I refer to as a need to win analysis. This analysis will help you to identify which side of the sales equation best matches you: hunter or farmer. Even within the hunter role, there are differences. The transaction-sale hunter, the one who sells something one time to a prospect, has a different reading than the complex-sale hunter.

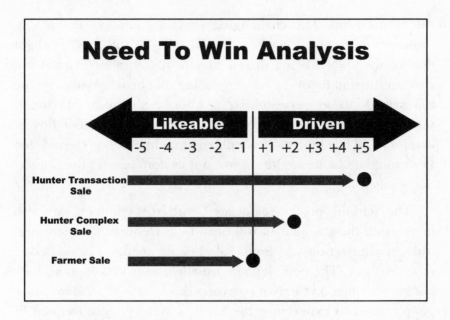

In a short, transaction-style sale, the drive of the salesperson is much higher than the need to be liked. In essence, this is a quick transaction with little future-selling opportunity. The salesperson, in a transaction sale, engages one or maybe two buying players. Their responsibility is less focused on building relationships and more on completing the sale. The buying cycle is usually short. Health-club sales and car sales are great examples of the transaction sale. Since the goal of this selling environment is to close the deal in the first meeting, the "drive" of the individual will be key to his success. If this person is more "likeable" than "driven," most will like the salesperson, but will buy from someone else. It is not that these salespeople shouldn't be likeable, just that they need to be significantly more predisposed to being driven.

In complex sales, this measurement is much more challenging. The complex salesperson deals with multiple buying players and the buying process is lengthy. Multiple phone calls and meetings usually occur during the course of the cycle. In this type of sale, the salespeople need to be likeable so that they can keep energy in the relationship. The challenging part of complex sales is that while the salesperson needs to be likeable, he still needs a slight dominance toward being driven to win. If the salesperson is not close to the middle of the scale, meaning that he is also likeable, he will struggle to be successful. He will not be able to build trusting relationships. Don't get me wrong: If he is more likeable than driven, everyone will like him, but few will buy from him. It is preferred that this candidate be more driven, just not as dominant as the transactional seller.

The lengthy process associated with the complex sale also means that the salesperson will not win as frequently as he would with the transaction sale. Some salespeople need to win every day, or every week. The complex sale usually means that winning happens a few times a year. Not everyone can handle that. Many salespeople need to experience the thrill of victory more frequently. Salespeople often try to fool themselves because they are again enticed by the almighty dollar. As this is a trait, the salesperson can rarely change this and failure occurs. Again, painful for all involved.

The big question to ask yourself is what type of buying cycle can you survive. Why do I call it surviving? By your very nature as a salesperson, you need the thrill of victory! Patience is not a virtue salespeople master. If *patience* is what we were after, we would all have become doctors. I've managed sales organizations that have had varying buying-cycle lengths. I've interviewed terrific salespeople who when they heard the buying cycle was twelve months or longer, discontinued the interview process. Imagine a sales cycle where it takes twelve months or longer to win. Granted, the win is about a half-million dollars in annual revenue, but still a long time for most to wait to taste success. And I appreciated that those candidates deselected themselves. They would have quit after three months of corporate investment and we both would have lost.

There are many salespeople who are accustomed to a longer process. They look at success at various intervals of the process rather than soley measuring themselves on winning the account. They use numerous metrics as part of their Sales Architecture to feel a more frequent win. If they scheduled an appointment with a key prospect, they felt a win. Others felt small wins as they moved through the cycle. This keeps them sane. It's like winning battles en route to winning the war. It takes a certain personal approach to be able to do this. If you are not cut out for a long buying cycle, do not be tempted by the gold at the end of the rainbow. You probably don't have what it takes to get there. I know that's a pretty aggressive statement, but remember, this book is for you. My goal is to make sure you make the best career choices for your own personal success.

Where Are the Leads?

Hunters also come in different breeds. Some hunters have historically created their own leads. Maybe they went door to door. Some may have just used the phone book. Other salespeople have generated new business for their company through company-created leads. These salespeople may have been given lead lists or answered inbound calls from prospects. There is an important distinction between these two types of hunters. When you consider your historical success, did you typically generate leads from scratch or did the company provide you with leads? These are both hunter roles, but the skills needed to be successful for each one is different.

I've seen many salespeople describe themselves as hunters and use the term broad-brush. As a manager, a mistake I made early in my career was not asking enough questions to identify the type of hunter skills the candidate possessed. As a result, I hired people who did not have the lead-generation skills which were a job require-ment. I heard "hunter," and did not dig deeper to see what type of hunter they truly were. Many of these salespeople failed as they could not jump-start their pipeline. They hadn't done it before and were not equipped to do it now. We both lost.

At the other end of the sales spectrum is the role of the farmer. For some reason, most salespeople think that the hunter is the sexy role. Quite frankly, many hiring managers do as well. They both miss the point. Farmers can play a key role in a sales organization. As a matter of fact, many salespeople are better suited to being farmers than hunters. Farmers have the core responsibility of selling additional products and services to existing clientele. This impor-tant function helps strengthen the relationship between the client and their respective company. Why is this role so important? The deeper the relationship is between two organizations, the more difficult it is to sever it. In the sales-trait analysis, farmers straddle the line between being likeable and being driven. Since they provide both a service and sales function, this spectrum balance is necessary.

Flexibility: Do You Bend or Break?

For example, think about your tolerance for change. Some may call this your ability to adapt. In some companies, things are very fluid. Titles change often, compensation plan structures change reg-ularly, and so on. Are you OK with that? Other companies offer a more stable environment. So how tolerant of change are you? Not everyone can handle the craziness of change. And you are fooling yourself if you think you can become more flexible. Yoga doesn't help with this type of flexibility. I know that I personally do not respond well to change. I prefer to have a clear understanding of what is expected of me and what I will earn for that performance. Sure, I might be able to earn more money somewhere else, but would I ever see those dollars? I'd probably quit in frustration before I saw my spike in income.

> **The better you can determine the environment in which you thrive, the greater your chance for selling success.**

Think about instances in your past when your flexibility was challenged. These examples are not limited to your professional career. It could be something as simple as a friend changing plans or your family moving across the country. How did you respond to this? How did you feel during the change? How did you feel after the change? Did you find a ray of sunshine in all of this change and you thus became more positive? Or did the change frustrate you? Try to come up with five examples and rank your flexibility on each one based on a 0–10 scale, with ten being the most flexible. Again, be honest with yourself. Average the numbers to see where you show a dominant pattern. Once you have found it, you will know your preference for your professional environment because at this stage of the game, your flexibility reading is probably not going to change. That's alright, just be mindful of this during your analysis. During the interview process, employers are rarely forthcoming about your need for flexiblity. An employer that is always in flux is not seen as a positive. Thus, a company is typically represented as a stable work environment. I've found the best way to ascertain the fluidity of the work environment is to speak to a few of the salespeople on the team. Questions about how long the present compensation plan has been in place, how long they have been in a particular role, and the frequency of territory change bring this out.

Looking Under the Hood

There are other considerations when formulating the profile such as:

Size of the company with respect to revenue: How big of a financial risk is this move for you? Is this a financially stable company or is there a possibility that your paycheck won't clear the bank? For public companies, this is easy to research. For private ones, it requires additional sleuthing. Private employers rarely tell you details of their financial performance. You can ask questions about their profit and growth, as that is a key indicator of success, but private firms won't share much. Do they have outside investors or is it a wholly owned firm? The idea is to know what you are getting yourself into. A high-risk company may have a better potential upside than a more stable one. The idea is for you to be able to make the best educated decision.

Size of company with respect to the competition: Are they a market leader or chasing one? Based on your history or your desires, you may decide that you are best-suited to sell for the market leader. Or, you may want to be the underdog going after the market leader. Some prefer the boutique environment that is more malleable to a client's needs. What was the size of your former employer relative to the competition? What size company do you want to sell for going forward?

Market position: Are they boutique or low-price? Other than in retail, I don't find many companies advertising that they are the low-price provider. That makes this a difficult aspect to ascertain in your evaluation. A good question to ask the employer is why they win and why they lose business. If they win because of price, that is a good indicator of market position. If they lose based on price, you know they are probably not a low-price provider. As a follow-up, it is helpful to know their approach to handling the price concern. If you don't buy it, how can you sell it? Have you sold for the low-price provider before? If you are considering the boutique, how will you make the transition?

You would think that market position is a question that would return a clear answer. This is not always the case. I can recall a lunch meeting I had with an executive of a large technology company. He was lamenting about sales management and team turnover. The team was not getting the results for which he had hoped. I asked what I thought would be a simple question for him to answer, "What are you selling?" After an elongated pause, he gave me what I can best describe as a clouded answer. It was apparent that he wasn't clear on what the products were and the areas of focus for the sales team. With that, I asked him how he thought his sales team could be successful if he didn't know what they should be selling. He got the point. If you encounter this, proceed with caution. How can you be successful if the organization isn't sure where they fit in the marketplace?

Breadth of offering: Is the offering comprehensive or part of a larger piece of the pie? With respect to the folks on whom you will call, what else do they buy? Is there a competitor who offers a more robust solution that includes this offering as a component? Or is this company offering the comprehensive solution? A great question to ask is how they differentiate themselves. Again, if you don't buy it, you probably can't sell it.

Sales management approach: How will sales success be measured? Micro versus macro management. Ah...another fan favorite. I don't think I ever interviewed a candidate who did not bring up the concern of micromanagement. In my experience, those who had the greatest concern for it needed it the most. The challenge is that many salespeople confuse performance expectation with micromanagement. Remember, for all of the dodo's flaws, she does want and need you to be successful. I've seen more salespeople hang themselves due to a lack of support than the other way around. My recommendation is to avoid the micromanagement discussion altogether. A healthier discussion is based on sales management expectations and support from the company. As a hiring manager, I became very concerned about any sales candidate's future when they shared concerns about micromanagement. However, I appreciated any candidate who wanted to understand my style, expectations, and the support I provided to the team.

Sales support: What are the tools available to help the sales team? For example, if the product has an ROI (return on investment), it would be helpful if the company had an ROI model for use with clients. If the sale is technical, who are the resources that help provide technical support? Does the company use a CRM (Customer-Relationship Manager) to help support the sales organization? How is the CRM used? Many of these tools reduce administrative burdens placed on the sales organization.

If you are a little perplexed as to how you can ascertain this information without offending the interviewer(s), you are not alone. It's tricky and delicate. It's not much different than conducting a needs analysis discussion with a prospect. Rapid-fire questions are not the way to go. Once you discern the most important elements of the job, you can determine which points are crucial to discuss early in the process. It's best to flush out the major points early so you don't waste your time pursuing a job that you don't want.

"Show Me the Money"

OK. Everything else about this opportunity matches well to your profile. Now it's time to consider money. In sales, the compensation plan serves as a mirror to a job description. Anyone looking at the plan will know what is expected of him. At least, this is the way it is supposed to work. Unfortunately, the world is not perfect and that does not always happen. You have probably heard that asking about money early in the interview process is considered a faux pas. As a hiring manager, I can tell you that I didn't care for it. However, I always appreciated those candidates who were trying to understand expectations and how compensation was tied to those expectations.

When the offer stage of the process was reached, I always provided the applicant a copy of the compensation plan and explained how the program worked. Oftentimes, applicants are quoted target incomes or provided with a conceptual overview of the compensation plan. Consider this path. You accept the job. On your first day, the compensation plan is shared with you. You have concerns with the plan. You have already quit your other job. You are stuck. This happens all the time with salespeople. You have a right to know how the plan works. It is not uncommon for salespeople to share compensation plans with an attorney to ensure the plan is mutually beneficial. Not to sound paranoid, but not all organizations are aboveboard in their handling of compensation.

There are also some terms with which I recommend you familiarize yourself.

Salary: This seems straightforward, but the term is not always used correctly. In sales, salary is usually money paid regardless of sales performance. It is not a loan against future commissions. It cannot be owed back to the company under any circumstances. Many states have specific laws addressing salaries for workers. You may want to research the laws of your state.

Recoverable draw: This is a loan against future commissions. Draws are usually put in place to help salespeople ramp up their earnings. It's meant to be an earnings bridge. Personally, I've never been a fan of the recoverable draw as it usually creates bad feelings between the salesperson and the company. It is rare that a draw period concludes and the salesperson does not have a debt to satisfy with the company. Who likes having debt? These programs can be structured in a variety of ways. Some companies will not pay any commissions until the entire draw is repaid. Others will allocate a percentage of commissions as repayment of the draw on a monthly basis. What you want to best understand is how the program works in this company. What is the history of salespeople with respect to draws? If you leave the company before the draw is repaid, what happens? These are great questions for your attorney when they review the plan.

Nonrecoverable draw: This program is the complete opposite of the recoverable draw. This is money provided to the salesperson without any expectation of repayment. But, be careful: While it is nonrecoverable, some companies do not pay commissions to their salespeople while they receive this draw. Others pay commissions if the commissions earned exceed the draw. Again, this is another important element for investigation.

Revenue: There are textbook definitions for gross revenue, net revenue, net profit, EBITDA, and so on. However, those definitions are not always followed when developing compensation plans. Whatever the metric, it is best to understand how that company defines the compensation-worthy elements. Revenue is a term that is utilized in different ways, in different industries, in different companies.

Chargebacks: Ah, the sneaky clause! Under certain circumstances, salespeople are asked for a return of their commissions. It could be because the client defaulted on payment. It could be that they were "slow payers." It could be because the client went bankrupt. You want to understand under what circumstances you could owe money back and for what timeframe. If this scenario plays out, how does the company handle it? Do they deduct it from the next paycheck? Is it done over time?

While some of this may seem taboo, you have an obligation to yourself to understand this as best as possible. Any businessperson will tell you that the best time to work on an agreement is while the relationship is still untarnished. I don't argue that you need finesse to do this, but any employer worth working for would appreciate the due diligence.

Deal Breakers

Deal breakers make-up the final part of the profile. These are the factors that you have determined are not acceptable under any condition. That said, it is easy to list these without an opportunity staring you in the face, but it is difficult to walk away from a prospective opportunity when it is within reach. In concept, this is fine. During the honeymoon phase, the deal-breaker is often a nonissue. In many instances, the issue gradually resurfaces over time if it was truly a deal breaker, and it becomes the ultimate death of the relationship.

Let's say you determined that a base salary of $40,000 is needed to meet your financial requirements as you start off in your new position. You participate in the interview process and everything is super, except for one thing. This employer will only start salespeople at $30,000. You can become blinded by the opportunity and accept the position despite the 25 percent shortfall. Now you've got the job. And guess where your focus is? You need to sell, and sell fast! Not only do you want to earn commission, you *need* to earn commission. You need the other $10,000 to survive. The toughest time to close a sale is when you need one.

This is a main disconnect between salespeople and employers. Employers think that hungry salespeople are great salespeople. However, there is a difference between survival and luxury. They would prefer to hire you at less than your desired or needed income so that you are motivated to sell. This is something that you are 100 percent accountable for avoiding. If you accept the job knowing the income doesn't meet your requirement, you are left to suffer the consequences.

One of the common deal breakers that I have seen a salesperson overlook is the acceptance of a position regardless of the commute time to the office. Many of them grow weary of the drive and look for other reasons not to stay. Everything else about the opportunity becomes negatively exaggerated. At the end of the day, the relationship crumbles and both the employer and salesperson lose. Just a thought, how will you explain this short tenure on your résumé to your next employer, since you accepted the job knowing that it took an hour and a half to get to the office?

Formulating Your Profile

Now, let's put all of this information to use. Based on what I shared in this chapter, formulate a profile of your ideal sales opportunity. This paints a clear roadmap of what you want and don't want. The job search is simply a matching game of the profile to the opportunity. Listed below is a partial topical list for consideration that will help identify the match. Once your profile is developed, you will probably add/edit the list. I highly recommend building this profile before you initiate your job search.

Historical
◆ What has made you successful in your prior sales experience?
◆ If you look at your experience, what do those past positions have in common?
◆ What were your responsibilities as a salesperson?
◆ Which did you enjoy?
◆ Which responsibilities did you not enjoy?
◆ Have you sold low-price or high-value products and services?

- Is your experience in selling tangible products, or services?

- How long was the buying cycle in your past experiences?

- Were your responsibilities more of a hunter or farmer?

- Were those sales types transactional or complex?

- From where did the leads come for the accounts you've won?

- Why do people buy from you?

Futuristic

- What do you want to learn from a new employer to further develop your skills?

- What is your tolerance for change?

- Do you want to sell for the market leader or the underdog going after the market leader?

- Do you prefer the large employer or the small/midsize one? How do you define employer size (revenue, employees, etc.)? Why is that important to you?

- Do you desire to sell a comprehensive solution or a specialized niche?

- Do you want to learn to sell something you haven't sold before?

- What sales support do you expect from the company?

Financials

- What are your financial requirements?

- What financial risks are you willing to take?

- ◆ What type of compensation structure is most palatable for you?
- ◆ What does the potential earnings increase need to be to justify making a change?

For all of these questions, it is important to ask yourself "why." If you prefer to sell for a large employer, why is that important to you? The idea is to be sure that you get your profile as focused as possible.

CHAPTER 3
Architecting Success

"Success means having the courage, the determination, and the will to become the person you believe you were meant to be."
—George Sheehan

Crazy Author

Hopefully, you have now determined that you are either working for the right company or have found a new opportunity that better suits you. Fantastic! You are in the right place. Now what? We've discussed that your sales manager is probably not equipped to help you with what you need to be successful. In a perfect world, on your first day, your manager handed you the roadmap for success, along with a structured training plan. That probably didn't happen, but they certainly do, however, ask you to produce results. How will you make yourself successful with little support from management? Drumroll, please! Introducing "Sales Architecture." I used the term earlier in the book, but now I will share with you how this applies to your selling world. After all, your success lies within you not your manager.

Sales Architecture is the clearly defined sales strategy, methodology, and process that supports your personal selling system. Why use a metaphor of architecture? Think of the development of a skyscraper. An architect develops the plan to ensure that the structure is sturdy and sound. The initial focus of the architect is to develop the foundation that supports this specific structure. Once that is determined, the architect creates the building's support structure that sits upon the foundation. At that point, careful consideration is given to the types of materials needed to support the designed structure. How tall will it be? What is the risk with high winds? If the wrong materials are chosen, the building will not be supported. Moreover, the foundation and support structure need to be in synch, as a support structure sitting upon the wrong type of foundation will ultimately collapse. The architect's job is complete upon the delivery of the plans for the building. Interestingly, his scope of responsibility does not include determining the color of the drapes for the windows of the office on the sixth floor. Truth be told, the concept of architecture was not my idea. Years ago, one of my salespeople noted that my approach was similar to that of an architect. She said, "You don't provide scripts. You teach concepts that allow me to use my own words to deliver the message my way. You simply provide a framework that helps me to be successful while allowing me to still be creative." I really appreciated that feedback and adopted that metaphor for my methodology.

> **Sales architecture is the sales framework that ensures a salesperson's success.**

You may think this is completely unnecessary. I can't blame you. If I were sitting where you are, I would be thinking the same thing: "I've been selling successfully for years and this guy is going to tell me how to do it? I don't think so." Or you may be thinking, "Am I really going to micromanage myself? I didn't want a manager who micromanages me, and now I'm going to self-inflict pain?" Don't worry; I'm up to your challenge. I'm used to presenting to sales professionals who greet me with folded arms and a wrinkled brow. By the time the presentation ends, the entire demeanor of the audience has changed to one of smiles and new-found confidence.

But you aren't there yet. You aren't sure why you bought this book in the first place. The humorous title may have led you to pick it up, but something else led you to buy it. So, let me address these concerns head-on. First, the concepts in this book would be difficult for a novice salesperson to apply to their selling approach. This is advanced-level stuff. If you haven't sold before, some of this will go right over your head. At the other end of the spectrum, this book will not provide you with a magical script that will double your sales. I often find that when salespeople read sales books or go to seminars, they have the unrealistic notion that they will learn the new recipe for water. They usually come away saying that they already knew all of what was presented, or it was a good refresher. I wouldn't waste your time with a refresher. Many of the concepts that I present are subtle, but you will see that subtlety can be the difference between success and failure in sales. They are nuances that will help you be more successful than you ever dreamed.

Secondly, this system is not about micro-management. It's an organizational support system that you will design based on what needs to transpire for you to be successful. Sales Architecture creates the sales support structure that facilitates your sales success. It is not about scripts, e.g., the curtains. Again, I don't believe in scripts. Selling is personal. You can't possibly feel passion when reading someone else's words. Any place in this book where dialogue is shown, it is 100 percent conceptual. It is not intended to be used at face value, nor is it intended to be memorized. The idea is that the concepts are incorporated into your personal selling style to formulate effective communication. This book will help you determine the right Sales Architecture for your specific selling landscape. If this were being taught in a classroom setting, the comparison of the participants' Sales Architecture would resemble the various buildings within a city's skyline. Some would be tall, others, short. Some would be wide, some, narrow. Some would have oblong windows, others, square. What they all have in common is that they are all sound structures. Sales Architecture includes the development of a foundation and five floors each with specific focal areas.

It is the concept of Sales Architecture that usually exposes the dodo sales managers. It's what's missing from most sales organizations. The dodo is usually unaware of the overall concept of this structure, but may try to incorporate pieces of it. The end result is usually a structure that is unsteady, unsophisticated, and dangerous. Not the intended result, but the result nevertheless. This is why many salespeople get frustrated. They feel like they are on the fifth floor of a building that is about to collapse! For the 90 percent of the salespeople in the limbo group I mentioned before, this instability keeps them awake at night. No Sales Architecture usually translates to failure for these folks. By incorporating this system, you will be able to become the eagle soaring majestically as the dodo looks to the sky in disbelief.

Foundation: Business Objective

The foundation of Sales Architecture is the overall business objective of the company. This can be learned by perusing annual reports for publicly traded companies. This direction is traditionally established at the C-level (chief-executive level). Employees are not always privy to the full picture of the objective, but key insight can be gained by reading the company's annual report, "10-Q," or just listening well in executive briefings. The compensation plan provides some key hints as well. As I shared earlier, the compensation plan for salespeople often doubles as a job description. What is the message that the compensation plan communicates? Sell big deals.

Sell small deals with a high margin. Sell a particular product. The compensation plan is a great tool to help derive this information. However, it is important to test what appears to be the message of the plan. Sometimes, there is a disconnect between the message the plan communicates and the goal of the company. Interviewing some company leaders is another way to understand the core objectives so that the system is based on a solid foundation. While the concept of the "foundation" may seem elementary, it is not. Just like the skyscraper, the foundation is the strength of the rest of structure. If the system is built based on increasing revenue, and the focus of the company is growing profits, the structure crumbles. The wrong prospects will have been selected for pursuit and the wrong strategy deployed.

Some companies are focused on increasing market share. They may trade profit dollars for an increase in market penetration. Others are focused on introducing a new product to the market. This may translate to their desire to pursue certain industries or specific companies. Some companies only want specific business at certain price points. Each of these affects how you get out of the gate. It is critical that you have directional clarity to be successful in defining your foundation.

1st Floor: Territory Management

Understanding the company's business objective paves the way for your construction of the structure as a whole. The first level is designed to identify the prospects for pursuit. No matter how big or small a given territory is, there are decisions to be made regarding the allocation of selling time. Since everyone works the same number of hours per day, it is important to identify how to best invest those hours. Which prospects to call and when, is the primary concept associated with establishing the first floor.

To make an effective time-investment determination, a methodology is needed to classify each of the potential prospects. In that methodology, every account gets classified in a way that helps focus your selling time. However, before these accounts can be classified, they need to be measured against what is defined as the ideal client. Sorry, I won't tell you who the ideal client is, but I will walk you through a process that helps you to determine that profile.

2nd Floor: Differentiation

With a prospect-identification model created, the next step is to determine messaging. How will you sound different than everyone else calling this company to sell their wares? Here's one of my favorites: "We are a market leader with the best service and leading-edge technology."

Truth is, I'm not sure if I have seen a salesperson who does not have this in his repertoire. I've always believed that if you can't prove it or demonstrate it, don't say it. Saying "best" without proof is meaningless vapor. It fails to create differentiation from the pack. Instead of helping to position "unique," it creates additional hurdles in the process, as your prospects have heard that expression from all of your competitors. Many salespeople use words like "unique" and "differentiator" without truly understanding their meanings or using them correctly. A hint: Look up the word "unique" in *Webster's Dictionary* prior to reading the chapter on differentiation.

> **Differentiation needs to be packaged in a meaningful way that buyers will accept and understand.**

Within this tier of the Sales Architecture, differentiation is identified and a communication plan is formulated. Communication is key, as each day, sales are lost due to the inability to communicate differentiation in a meaningful way. To aid communication with the buying community, a sound-byte is developed. This serves as a tool for message communication. Sorry folks, marketing cannot do this for you. Again, selling is personal. But don't fret; there is a workshop in this chapter that walks you through how to build this. Since each salesperson has their own unique style, how the story is told will be different for each of you. However, the same framework is used for all.

3rd Floor: Buying Players

Since selling is an exercise facilitated among people, it is critical to understand how they think. On this floor, each of the potential buyers, whom I refer to as "buying players," is profiled to understand how to best communicate with them. These folks affect the buying decision with varying roles and influence in the process. I present a different approach for identifying the four key buying players that exist in every opportunity, with the focus on finding the key player: "The Mentor". The Mentor is the key to every win. Characteristics of a strong Mentor, developing that buying player into a strong Mentor, and helping him to overcome obstacles are all new responsibilities that I establish for salespeople as part of this new approach.

Profiling each of the buying player roles that are encountered is another component of this floor. This allows the customization of the developed message (sound-byte) for each of the buying players so it is tied to their goals and challenges, as well as spoken in their language. Also, with that information at hand, strategies can be developed for working with each of them in the most effective manner.

4th Floor: The Buying Process

Buying process? It's a sales process...isn't it? Nope. The role of the salesperson is to facilitate the buying process so the buyers feel empowered and in control. As Jeffrey Gitomer says, "People don't like to be sold-but they love to buy." Think about that for a moment. The thought of buying a new car is exhilarating, but the experience is miserable, as a salesperson will act more as a sales barrier than a facilitator. The health club industry analyzed when people decided to join a club. What they found was unbelievable. The majority of people made the decision to join before they ever entered the club. The salesperson somehow "sells" them out of joining. This is a very important consideration for you as you continue on with this reading.

Being the facilitator of the buying process, sometimes it means you ask questions. At other times, it is a listening exercise. Still other times, information is shared. The trick is when and how this is done, with consideration of the buyer's needs. This is a major perspective shift for many salespeople as "sales process" is a standard term and concept. However, "sales process" places focus on the wrong side of the equation. To effectively facilitate the buying process, a deep understanding of the buyers is needed. When they say something, what are they truly trying to communicate?

In essence, the salesperson's role is to facilitate the dialogue of interest. This includes needs analysis, presentation, and utilization of appropriate tools. A step-by-step process is presented to formulate a powerful needs analysis program that gathers the information needed for the process and differentiates with the buying community. Through the use of various questions and positioning, the buying players will be engaged in a way that they will find different. A deeper, more meaningful rapport will be developed with buying players than has ever been experienced before.

Great stuff! Can't miss, right? Wrong! There will be defects in the process. Deals will still get stuck in the pipeline. That, I can assure you. So another aspect of this is the development of a plan to resolve concerns, manage references, position pilots, and more. In essence, things will go left of center, let's have a plan to address them when they do.

5th Floor: Personal Growth

One thing that can be counted on is that the competition will get better each and every day. Today's easy win is tomorrow's loss, unless a personal-development plan is in place. How are you going to constantly improve? How will you better yourself on a daily basis? It takes commitment to do it.

Consider this. Albert Einstein formulated the theory that says that space and time are relative concepts rather than absolute ones. For example, consider a car-speedometer reading of 65 miles per hour. How fast is the car going? This question seems like the beginning of the joke of who is buried in Grant's tomb, where a punch line is expected. No joke here, I assure you. As a matter of fact, most would respond, "65 miles per hour." This is the correct answer if, and only if, it is a comparison to a car that is not moving. However, comparing that same car to a car driving 55 miles per hour next to it, the car is only moving at 10 miles per hour.

So, what does that have to do with sales? When looking at your sales performance, to what standard do you compare yourself? Is it to the others on the sales team? Is it to your sales quota? Is it to a sales record that has stood for ten years in your company? Maybe you look at your performance relative to your income goals.

While any of these comparative points are important, they all have one thing in common: They limit your potential. How good can you be? If a ceiling is set, you may never know. Yes, hitting quota is important. Achieving income goals is also important. But could more be achieved? Is "better" possible? The car moving at 65 miles per hour is moving pretty fast, but only relative to a nonmoving entity. Your competitors are moving right along with you. Maybe you are in the lead today, but competition does not stagnate. To them, maybe you are only moving at 10 miles per hour.

Compare that same car to a jet. The speed of the car is not overly impressive. The jet can commute from New York to Florida in a couple of hours. The car needs 24 hours to reach the same destination. Competitors get smarter. Buyers become more educated. What worked yesterday is not going to work tomorrow. Self-improvement is the only way to do it.

There are no ceilings in sales unless someone constructs them. One of my favorite quotes is, "When someone says it can't be done, it only means that *he* can't do it." Every day people accomplish the seemingly impossible. How do they do it? Simple: they do not compare themselves to any standard. They have no limitations. As I write this, I'm flying on a plane. If the Wright brothers believed in ceilings, I'd be driving. If Bill Gates believed people would never own a personal computer, I'd be writing this on a typewriter.

To further make this point, I thought I would share a personal story. When I was in the eighth grade, my family moved from New York to New Jersey. At the time we moved, I was an excellent student, A's across the board. Shortly after moving, I injured my knee playing baseball. I had two knee surgeries and spent my entire freshman year of high school on crutches. There I was, living in a new state, going to a new school, knowing next to no one. I lost my focus.

I became friendly with a few kids who were not very good students. They were nice kids, not troublemakers, but they did not perform well in school. During my freshman year of high school, I set my personal-worst record for grades, but I was able to rationalize my performance. My grades were nothing to write home about, but I was scoring better than my friends. From that relative point of view, I was doing fine.

Toward the end of my freshman year, I became friends with a different group of kids. These friends later attended Wharton, Harvard, Emory, and Bates, all prestigious schools. Relative to them, my grades were a disgrace. They never made me feel badly about it, but I felt uncomfortable. Their success drove me to rediscover myself. During the remainder of my high school and collegiate career, I elevated my game to top of the class. I credit much of that with changing my approach to relativity.

Nature also uses the theory of relativity. If you put a fish in a 10-gallon tank, the fish will only grow to a certain size. The surroundings of the fish limit its size and growth. Put that same fish in a larger tank and the fish will continue to grow. Want to get better at golf? Play with better golfers. Want to run faster? Train with better runners.

What limitations are you putting on your sales success? Are you failing to achieve your quota? Are your friends on the team missing their quota too? Do you accept that because you are all failing? Or do you compare yourself to a higher standard? What are you doing each and every day to improve yourself? Is your goal just to be better, or is it to be the best?

Some salespeople focus on pleasing their manager. They spend their time worrying about corporate gossip and rumors. Other salespeople look at everyone in their company as working for *them*. This is not an ego statement, but rather a mental position. Regardless of the company, every salesperson is running a business. All of the employees in the company are resources to make sure their business is successful. This may seem like common sense, but I hear more salespeople focused on pleasing the company than running their business. As long as the business objectives are the same or greater than the corporate ones, this is probably not going to be an issue. It does help position, however, one's psyche for what needs to get done.

This entire book is tied to a salesperson's personal development. If you've read this far, I'm assuming that you are committed to personal development and improvement. The concepts presented require an open mind and an investment of time to work. Again, I'm here to help you through it.

CHAPTER 4
So Many Selling Opportunities, So Little Time

"He who finds diamonds must grapple in mud and mire because diamonds are not found in polished stones. They are made."

—Henry B. Wilson

Big Rocks

I wish I had a magical way to add more hours to the day. I really do, but I can't. That leaves us all to be dealt the same hand of 24 hours with which to accomplish our goals. The key is what one elects to do with that time which determines their success or failure. One of the interesting aspects of the sales profession is that it is very easy to be busy all the time, and yet, still fail to accomplish the tasks most critical for sales success. Tasks come from every direction and at the end of each long day, exhaustion is the only thing that is felt. The question is: "What was truly accomplished today?" Those who are honest with themselves understand that there are many days that they were really busy, but accomplished little in the way of the critical sales activities that make them successful.

Steven Covey writes about time management in his book *First Things First*, using a metaphor of big rocks, pebbles, sand, and water. (It's a great read and one I highly recommend if you are time management challenged.) An allegory is shared about a fish tank. The rocks, pebbles, and sand are each placed in the tank in that order. Covey asks after each item is placed in the tank if the tank is now full.

He explains that placing the big rocks in first, followed by pebbles, sand, and water is a metaphor for time. The most critical items to be added are the big rocks. He further proposes inverting the equation whereby the water is poured in first. No room for the big rocks, or the pebbles, or sand, for that matter. In essence, the day can be full without the main priorities being addressed.

> **Time is a precious resource.**
> **Manage it wisely.**

But what are the big rocks for a salesperson? If success is based on having a healthy sales pipeline, then activities related to that are the big rocks. In this example, the exercise of prospecting is a big rock, or actually, a boulder. Without prospecting, the pipeline dries quickly. In my experience, most salespeople would rather let a boulder roll over them than prospect. It's not fun, but it is critical for sales success.

The same fish-tank metaphor can be applied to a sales territory. Maybe the territory has been defined as a city, or a few cities, or even a region of states. Maybe the turf is a list of accounts. Perhaps, no defined territory has been provided at all, just an instruction to go sell to the world. Regardless, every account can't be pursued at the same time. Interestingly, in many complex sales, the amount of selling effort required to win a small deal is about the same as a large one. However, many salespeople focus on the little opportunities, thinking that quota will be achieved through a volume of wins. This rarely happens because there are only a certain number of selling hours in the day, and the size of the wins does not add up to achieve the goal. This makes territory management an important part of the Sales Architecture structure. Regardless of what hand has been dealt for a territory, it falls on the salesperson to prioritize it in a meaningful way.

Many salespeople have come to the realization that they do not get rewarded for hard work. That said, many work too hard—much harder than is necessary to be successful. The winners of the sales game are those who think, plan, and strategize more than they execute. The old methods—the right arm of many—of using a simple mathematical equation of leads to calls to sales is not enough to make one successful when selling in today's world. Now, the sales game is different in regard to the people, the way people buy, and so on.

Wait a minute. Did the game really change, or have salespeople played it incorrectly since the beginning of time? When I examined the methods that salespeople use to select prospects for their selling time, I saw two consistent themes. The large majority of salespeople utilized a shotgun approach to selling that I refer to as "Spreading." At the other end of the spectrum, there were those who took a sharpshooter approach, which is referred to as "Digging."

The shotgun seller (Spreader) is unfocused. This salesperson tries to sell pieces and parts of a solution to as many prospects as he can locate. There is no commonality in the prospects. Spreading is a very common approach in selling today. It focuses on the theme of safety in numbers. "If I am working with 200 companies, something has to close." Those who use this strategy work very hard and, most often, earn significantly less than the Digger. The Spreader does not create a unique strategy for each account, but rather a standard product pitch. This is sometimes called "dialing for dollars." The Spreaders usually fail because it is impossible to be dedicated to the pursuit of so many accounts. These salespeople get little pockets of business from many organizations, but remain envious of those who outperform them with just a handful of accounts. For the complex sale, the Spreader approach, while pursued by many, usually results in frustration and failure.

By contrast, the Digging approach, of selling a complete solution, to a well-defined prospect, inclusive of all of the products and services within their scope makes better sense. The sharpshooter pursues prospects who meet a specific series of criteria and focuses on selling the entire solution to the prospect. The list of criteria helps to formulate the definition of the ideal client. This will be discussed at length later in the book.

Diggers pursue the ownership of an entire account for all solutions their organization provides. It means that their focus is on a finite list of accounts with the goal of total conquest. Comprehensive strategic and tactical plans are developed to fully understand what is required to earn the business. Research on each account is performed to understand their buying culture and a constant following of the changes in their client's business is maintained.

The Diggers become experts in their client's business. Metaphorically speaking, these are the "gold diggers," who are convinced that they have found the spot where the treasure is located. They are unfazed by failing to locate the gold during their initial dig, and won't move to another spot until they have unearthed every pebble to make sure they don't miss out on finding the gold.

The Spreader has three main flaws when compared to the Digger. The first is the failure to identify his ideal-client criteria. This salesperson pursues any and all potential prospects. Many of the pursuits end in disappointment, as the prospect was not really a match. The second flaw is that he is not maximizing their selling time. Pursuit of all prospects, qualified and unqualified, causes a tremendous amount of wasted motion. The third flaw is that there is not a focus on growing the selling opportunity within an account. Account vulnerability is created, as a provider with a more robust solution can win it all. Senior executives know that they lose buying power and consistency when multiple solutions are deployed within their organization. In addition, most organizations are trending toward reducing their provider population. At some point, central standards will be pursued, leaving some providers out of the game. You don't want that to be you.

Interestingly, parents constantly tell their children to finish what is on their plate and then, and only then, can they have more. If the same philosophy were adopted for selling, salespeople would sell a prospect a solution and continue the selling initiative within that organization until the comprehensive solution was sold, or was dead.

Don't get me wrong about metrics in sales; algorithms are an important benchmark in sales performance. They help identify successes and areas for improvement. However, these are not the only determiners of success. What if a salesperson was making calls and generating appointments, but the buyers turned out to be unqualified? Wasted sales time. Territory management helps to ensure that the algorithms are meaningful. With that in mind, the process that is described in the rest of this chapter will help to ensure that the prospects with whom selling time is invested are the best ones for the investment. One other factor is that the salary that companies pay is for your time. They own these minutes, which means they are expecting a wise investment of the resource. The territory management-system component of your Sales Architecture is designed to ensure that the right prospects are pursued at the right time. However, to be able to set those priorities, the ideal client needs to be defined.

The Ideal Client

There are a number of criteria that shape the definition of the ideal client. Again, the goal is to be able to identify the best opportunities for pursuit at the right time. Some criteria to consider are:

Size: How *large* of a prospect will you pursue? But what is the definition of large? Based on the type of sale, size can be defined in a variety of ways. For example, a salesperson who sells employee benefits may define size by the number of employees in a company. The copier salesperson may define size based upon the number of copiers that the company might purchase. Many salespeople confuse small sales for short buying cycle.

Circumstance: Does the prospect use this solution today or must a need be developed? There are certain industries that require salespeople to create demand for their product. Their clients are first-time adopters. Think of the Blackberry®. A few years ago, this was new technology, and their salespeople were required to build a business case for prospects to purchase this tool. Other industries are based upon "takeaway" business, which means that the prospect already uses a similar product or service. The goal of the salesperson, in this scenario, is to build a business case that concludes with the prospect purchasing from *him* instead of the competition.

Some salespeople confuse these two types of circumstances and the result is often painful. The buying cycle becomes protracted if one tries to create demand in a mature market. In this case, the purchasing community has, for the most part, determined their interest. Thus, it is very difficult to change that. A great example of this is the market for employee drug testing. Most of the Fortune 1,000 employers use this service. Those who don't drug test their employees made the business decision not to adopt this screening tool. Therefore, it is a very difficult, and rarely success-ful, venture for the salesperson to convince the organization to adopt it.

Process: What is the right time for the salesperson to enter the process with respect to effective differentiation and a reduced buying cycle? This is very tricky, as it always helps if the prospect is in the process of considering a provider change. However, this may make it more difficult to facilitate the buying process in a way that allows for differentiation. Some buying processes yield winning results when the salesperson generates the initial interest to begin the process of a provider change. The salespeople are able to differentiate them-selves, and buyers are receptive to listening to creative solutions. In other scenarios, the receipt of a request for proposal (RFP) is the best way to proceed.

> ## Applying the profile of the ideal client ensures the right opportunities are pursued at the right time.

Budget: What budget does a prospect need to have set aside for this purchase? This also correlates to "size," but takes it one step further. This accounts for the dollars needed to acquire the product or service. If the business is takeaway, some dollars are allocated, but not necessarily enough for a more robust solution. If this is new adoption business, dollars need to be created for the investment. In many cases, return-on-investment (ROI) tools are needed to justify the sale. If dollars need to be created, this may protract the buying process, making this prospect less of a focus than one that already has the budgeted dollars. What is the required investment for your solution?

Buying Habits: Where is the offering priced relative to the marketplace? Hyundai-buyers don't typically buy Mercedes. If a prospect strictly buys on price, the probability that they will deviate from that pattern is low unless the product is heavily differentiated. It doesn't make sense to pursue those accounts. This is sometimes identified by how purchasing decisions are made. If every product or service is procured through an RFP (request for proposal), then there is cause for concern, as they may be primarily price buyers.

Territory Management System

With a clear definition of the ideal prospect, the next step is to apply that definition to your territory. There is a five-step process that will provide a focus for the territory. The first three phases of the process focus on analyzing the territory with the goal of formulating a list of accounts, which I refer to as "Targets." Targets represent the best sales opportunities in the territory that meet the definition of the ideal client. A secondary list is also formulated called "Horizons." Horizons are the next ten best opportunities in the region. In essence, a roster of accounts is developed, with a watchful eye on another ten. The concept is very similar to sports. In baseball, the manager may *love* forty seven players, but can only have twenty five on the active roster. The management of the team has to make tough decisions to get to the twenty five limit. Teams have no more, and no fewer than the twenty five. For purposes of this exercise, I will use twenty-five as the roster limit for Targets, but that number may need to be adjusted based on your type of sale. A word of caution: Many salespeople make the list so large that they become Spreaders.

Depicted is the process for territory management that will help to develop that roster of twenty-five Targets, with a plan to pursue each.

Phase 1 – Identification

I've touched a few times on the point that not every company is the right company to pursue. Others are the right company, but the timing is not the best to pursue them. Not every company is a prospect. The standard industry term for the overall group of companies in a given territory is "Suspects." With a list in hand of all of the Suspects in the territory, the process begins by classifying each using the Prospect-Identification Model. The model presents rankings from A1 to D3. These classifications are not permanent and, most likely, will change over time. The core concept behind the use of this model is to help to determine the best prospects to pursue and when. It is a key element to being able to manage your most precious resource, your time. The "identification phase" concludes with the production of the Target list.

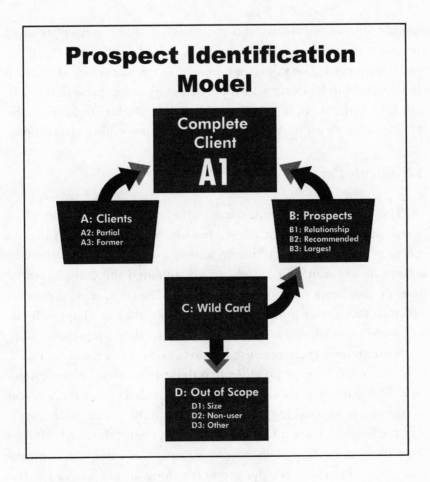

A: Client Relationships

The "A" group has a revenue relationship associated with it. Either the account is purchasing products and services from the provider, or has done so in the past. There are also three subclasses within this "A" group.

A1: Client- Complete

In a perfect world, every account would buy everything that a provider has to offer. It is an admirable goal, but not necessarily a realistic one. Those clients who are classified as "A1" have purchased the comprehensive solution to meet their needs, and the account has been conquered. The sales bag is empty! In essence, there is no additional selling to be done with these accounts at the present time. If, and hopefully when, a provider adds a new product or service, the A1s can drop down to A2 as there may be a new selling opportunity.

A2: Client- Partial

This category represents clients who have purchased part of an overall solution, but for whatever reason, use multiple providers to meet their needs. Ouch! Simply stated, a provider can be further serving an account, but has either not pursued the complete solution, or has been rebuffed while trying. This is a great group on which to focus your sales effort. Presumably, they are happy clients and would welcome the conversation to further the relationship. Many companies recognize the benefits, both service and financial, of having a sole source provider that delivers a comprehensive solution. The burden is on the salesperson to convert this recognition into action to expand the relationship. From the provider's perspective, the broader the solution delivered to a client, the harder it is to sever the relationship. This becomes important when the competition comes knocking on the account's door and offers to cut the provider's price by 5 percent. With client entanglement, the cost of change can easily exceed 5 percent, which further protects the provider's business. Every provider has a bad day. With a broad solution in place, the client will need to partner with the provider to get through it instead of simply finding someone else to do the work.

A3: Client- Former

This category represents those with whom a prior business relationship existed. However, the client stopped buying from the provider for any of a myriad of reasons. The key is that his business is still desired by the provider. The obvious question here is, why rank the pursuit of former business so high? People change and circumstances change. There is tremendous gold to be mined in former clientele, but it is usually left unmined.

Often, salespeople convince themselves that there is no way to ever bring that client back. In some cases, that may be a true statement. However, consider the following scenario. A small provider loses a client because it did not have the resources to provide the desired levels of service. That small provider is acquired by a multimillion-dollar firm that is committed to growing that provider's business. A tremendous opportunity now exists to revisit that client's business, as it is now possible to satisfy their more comprehensive needs. That said, how many salespeople would pursue that client? In many sales minds, they are gone, never to return.

In another scenario, the relationship with the key buying player may have soured. Some of the issues were the provider's, but others were the client's. That buying player leaves the organization, clean-slate. Again, how many salespeople track these A3 opportunities?

Still another scenario: The client leaves the provider for one who offers a cheaper solution. We've all made the mistake of buying cheap and going back to the original provider.

OK, one more scenario: The client is acquired, and the provider of the acquiring company is selected to provide services. The provider wasn't at fault; it just did not have a relationship with the acquiring firm to hold on to the business. Why not pursue the acquiring company and use the other group as a reference?

B: Prospect

Remember the discussion of the ideal client? This is where that definition gets applied. The "B" group encompasses those prospects that meet the criteria of the ideal client, but have never purchased anything from the provider. Within the "B" group, there are three subgroups.

B1: Prospect- Relationship

This is a prospect whereby the salesperson, someone within his company, or a business partner has a prior relationship. This is the best prospect to pursue because there is a level of trust already established. Established trust accelerates the buying process and puts that provider in the lead for the business. Thinking about how I make buying decisions, I always prefer to work with someone I, or trusted friends, already know. If that trust exists, the prospect is less likely to "shop the business."

B2: Prospect- Recommended

This subclass of prospects includes those who a knowledgeable person has recommended for pursuit. Many salespeople are working for companies that have existed for many years and other salespeople have been assigned historically to their territory. Why start from scratch? What is the history in the territory? Who knows the history? Conversations with the right people in the company may yield additional "A3s" to the list too. It's common to find that there was meaningful dialogue with a prospect, but for whatever reason, the process cooled and no one followed-up.

B3: Prospect- Largest

Yes, size matters, particularly in sales. The "B3" group is made up of the largest prospects who meet the criteria of the ideal client. As mentioned before, the salesperson has to apply his own definition of size to determine the "largest." However, these are the largest who have not already been classified in earlier, higher-ranking categories. They are not purchasing from this supplier, nor have they ever purchased anything from the supplier. The salesperson doesn't have an established relationship, nor is he aware of anyone with buying influence. No one has recommended them, either. To provide you with a visual, a salesperson is driving down the highway and sees a huge office building with a name on it. He sets a goal of converting that company into a client. In more practical terms, a salesperson reviews a Hoover's list to get this information.

C: Wildcard

Since every company needs to be classified, those about whom not enough information is known are listed as "wildcards." Little research has been conducted to determine the true opportunity that lies within this suspect. Further analysis will result in a classification of "prospect" or "out of scope." It is common to have a lot of these when a salesperson is assigned a territory. Over time, there will be fewer and fewer of these in the portfolio.

D: Out of Scope

The "D" classification is set in place to categorize those who do not meet the definition of the ideal client. There are three sub-groups within the "D" classification that provide reasons why they don't meet the criteria. This is not a death sentence for these Suspects. The statuses can and will change over time. Don't forget about these guys! As a supplier's capabilities and goals evolve, today's "D" is tomorrow's "B."

D1: Out of Scope- Size

The D1 subclass is assigned to those Suspects who are too small to justify the investment of a salesperson's time. I've hit this one a few times. The hours are precious; you can't invest in those oppor-tunities that don't have an adequate return.

D2: Out of Scope- Nonuser

This group is comprised of those Suspects who do not have use for the supplier's products or services. Salespeople often abuse this category. There is a major difference between a salesperson being unable to get in the door of a company, and a company who has been well-informed of a particular solution. Those companies have made the business decision not to adopt that type of solution in their environment. To explain further, imagine you were selling bathroom towel dispensers that work off of a motion sensor. If you presented this product to the office manager and procurement and as a result of those discussions, they made the decision not to incorporate this technology into their bathroom, the account would be classified as a D2. However, if a meeting cannot be scheduled or a meaningful dialogue has not taken place, that company is best listed in a more appropriate category to match the circumstance, including the "wildcard" one.

D3: Out of Scope- Other

For some reason other than size and nonuser, the provider does not desire the Suspect's business. Maybe it is an organization within an industry in which the provider has not established a presence. It could be that the provider knows that there are certain elements required for a particular industry's solution and they don't offer those products and services. It could be that the Suspect is rumored to be acquired/merged. For example, if a salesperson were trying to sell services to airlines, they would probably avoid the ones which have been in the newspaper lately because of mergers or acquisitions. The timing is probably not right for a healthy buying process, at least not when there are better opportunities in the territory to pursue.

Phase 2 – Selection

With all of the Suspects and prospects classified, the "Identification" phase is complete. The next phase becomes "Selection," whereby the Target and Horizon lists are formed. The classifications become the cornerstone of the list's development. The A1s are not added to the list since there is nothing more to sell them, at least not now.

The first group added to the Target list is the A2s since it is easiest to leverage existing business relationships. From there, the A3s who the salesperson feels can be won back are added. With the remaining slots, the prospects (Bs) are added. First, the B1s, then the B2s, and finally, the B3s. Using the requirement of twenty-five slots, the roster is probably overflowing.

At this point, the salesperson needs to make some tough decisions and cut those who are not as good as the other twenty-five. It's tough! With the criteria for the ideal client at your side, each "Target" is compared to those criteria to determine the best ones. The next ten best are classified as "Horizons." The Horizons are those who meet the criteria of the ideal client, but aren't as strong as the others who made the Target list. Horizons can be promoted to Targets and Targets demoted to Horizons as business is won or lost.

At the other end of the spectrum, some salespeople may not have filled out their roster. It's very common when a new salesperson joins a company for this to happen. This simply means that additional research is needed in the territory to identify Suspects that are really Prospects (Bs). They need more information to incorporate this process into their world. Research of Hoover's, or other account-information source lists will help. Dialogue with company executives will also help. Ask sales peers. Research into the company CRM for territory history can also prove invaluable.

I've had some sales managers say that they want to give their salespeople the account priority list. It's certainly their decision to make, but I give them a moment of pause with one question. Who is passionate about the list that has been formulated? The answer is the sales manager. However, the pursuit of the business is left to the salesperson. I've always left this exercise to be driven by the salespeople, but collaborated with them so they would have the best possible list. I established the goal of having my team members wake up each day excited and focused on the list of clients whom they determined to be the best opportunities to pursue.

With the twenty-five identified, a matrix like the one depicted is created as the next phase, "Strategic Planning," commences. The salesperson inserts the company, ID, date listed, first-meeting date, last-meeting date, and last-contact date into the appropriate columns. The others are completed during "Strategic Planning."

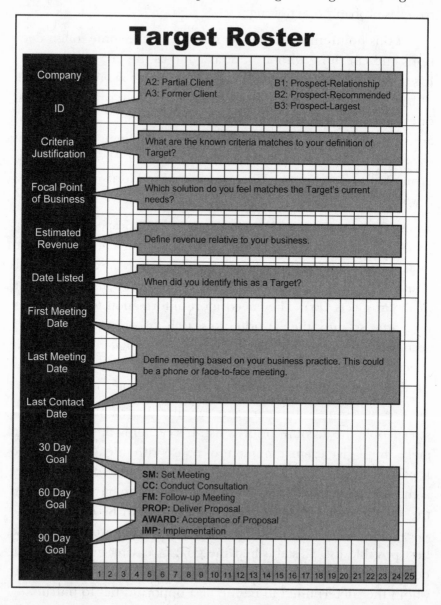

Phase 3 – Strategic Planning

Since the Target list has been formulated, the next step is to develop a strategic plan to pursue each of those Targets. The first question to ask is why you are passionate about each of these. It is most powerful if it is tangible. For example, if a salesperson selected Exxon Mobil for pursuit, the criteria justification could be his experience in selling to the oil sector, the other clients he has in the oil sector, and/or a creative solution he has for the oil sector. The idea is to have a strong, tangible reason to go after this particular company to expand or commence doing business. For each Target, the salesperson inserts his criteria justification in the matrix. Hey, they got on the list! There has to be a great reason for it. They beat out hundreds, if not thousands, of other accounts.

The next step is to determine a focal point of business. Which of the supplier's products and services are expected to be of interest to this Target? If a salesperson were selling copiers, a major corporation is probably not going to be interested in the slowest, cheapest copier they have. So, which copier probably best matches this type of company? The focal point of business is inserted in the matrix for each Target.

The salesperson is passionate about each account and knows which products and services make the most sense for each Target. The next step is to formulate an action plan for each with 30–60–90-day goals. Each plan is unique to account for the varying situations. Those actions may be: set a meeting, conduct a consultation, conduct a follow-up meeting, and present a proposal. These are followed by acceptance of the proposal and implementation. Those 30–60–90-day goals are inserted into the matrix. Oftentimes, salespeople overstate their goals for the time period. A reality check is needed to ensure the plans for each, and in total, are feasible for the respective time period.

Also during this phase, buying players (those who would be involved in a purchasing decision) and strategic partners are identified. In essence, a roadmap is developed which depicts the plan to convert the "Target" into an "A1" client.

Phase 4 – Execution

There have been a number of studies published on why CEOs fail. The most common reason is not that a poor plan was developed, but rather a failure to execute it. "Execution" is the deployment of the strategy that was developed during the "Planning" phase. This is when the game is played. The main goal to be achieved during this phase is for the salesperson to implement the plan developed in the prior phase. The proper execution of this phase results in the specified goals being attained. In essence, it continues to show forward movement with the account.

> **Being passionate about the pursuit of an account is a key ingredient to a salesperson's success in formulating their Target list.**

Many salespeople like this phase the most, as they can compare their daily activities to their Target list and feel a sense of accomplishment. It keeps their day focused. Salespeople often ask me if these are the only prospects on whom to call. I spin the question back to them by asking if they have selected the right roster size for their business type. If they answer "no," I encourage them to revisit the roster size. If they answer "yes," then my question for them is: If they are passionate that these are the best opportunities to pursue, why would they want to call anyone else?

Phase 5 – Reflection

Probably the area most overlooked by salespeople is that of "reflection." This is a regular, periodic analysis of strategic planning and execution. What was the plan? Was it completed? Did the plan work?

During this phase, the salesperson reviews the 30-day milestone versus achievement, ensures 60-day milestones are on track, and develops new 90-day milestones based on activities from the past 30 days. This is also the opportunity to make changes to the "Target" list. The two reasons for making changes to this list are conversions to "A1" and lost optimism about a selection. Dropping accounts from this list will be kept to a minimum if Phases 1 and 2 were performed well. Dramatic changes to this list are cause for review. It's either great news because all of the opportunities have been converted to A1 status, or, more commonly, the salesperson did not perform thorough due diligence in the selection phase. This causes a tremendous amount of waste time and motion by the salesperson.

There are a few ways to conduct Reflection. One way is to collaborate with the sales manager. If nothing else, sales managers are usually good salespeople, which makes them a good resource for this exercise. Another option is to find a peer, a sales buddy, and you can do this together. For this to work, you both must agree to be completely candid with your comments. If sales buddies just congratulate each other, the session is wasted time, time that cannot be wasted.

This is all about accountability. The plan falls down if salespeople don't hold themselves accountable for delivering against their goals. Yes, their goals. They set the goals and they need to achieve them. As a manager, it is always an interesting exercise to confer with salespeople during "Reflection" to see if they delivered performance against their goals. I didn't set these. They did. It made for a very different discussion than if I had set the goals for them. I've found over the years that people are more likely to achieve goals they've set themselves versus goals set by others. I hold salespeople accountable for having goals, but they have to determine the right goals. I provided coaching when asked to and challenged the salesperson to make certain he had the best, most realistic goals set.

Personal accountability is needed for this process to work. If the salesperson does not hold himself accountable for delivering in each of the five phases, the whole system fails. There is no short-changing the results. It's like the guy who runs on a treadmill for an hour every day and eats Hostess Twinkies as a diet staple: not going to see results.

CHAPTER 5
The Secret of How Buyers Buy

"Knowing others is intelligence; knowing yourself is true wisdom.
Mastering others is strength; mastering yourself is true power."

—Unknown

The Buyer's Game

As I shared earlier, the process facilitated by a salesperson is called a buying process, not a selling process. But how can a salesperson facilitate a buying process if they don't know how buyers buy? In essence, how does the procurement process work? How does this company make buying decisions? With that understood, a successful strategy can be formulated.

Many large companies have adopted formal-buying processes. These are often managed by the Procurement Department. In formal-buying settings, the process usually begins with the Procurement Agent working with the users (those requesting assistance in purchasing) to determine the scope of their needs. Once the scope is identified, the procurement agent formulates a Request for Information (RFI) or Request for Proposal (RFP). The document is sent to a list of what they call vendors (a term that is about a big an insult as a salesperson can receive), which is determined in one of two ways: The users provide a list of requested respondents, or procurement selects vendors from their own research.

> **Buyers try to create sameness when buying for their best negotiating position.**

Typically, a small group of respondents (commonly called finalists) is asked to make a presentation to a buying committee based on the RFI/RFP submissions. After the presentation, the committee elects to negotiate pricing with one or two of the finalists, and an award is ultimately made. Buying situations vary, however, with some buying decisions being made exclusively on the RFP response from the vendors. This is often the case in a government-buying process.

In the last few years, a new final step has been added to the process: electronic auctions, also called "e-auctions." Unlike most auctions you may have experienced where the price goes up like on eBay, these auctions are designed to bring the price down and create commodity. These online auctions take price slashing to new levels. Studies performed by the professional purchasing organizations support the use of these e-auctions. It's a very scary fate if adoption of this technology continues to grow.

Rather than a traditional negotiation exercise being conducted, the finalist group is requested (yeah, *requested*) to participate in an online-auction event. An auction date is set and the auction lasts for a set duration, usually one hour. Often times, these auctions do not show competitors' prices, but show rank in contrast to the other bidders. The simple objective of the procurement folks is to drive the price down.

Pathetic! Makes some want to exit sales, not invest in it. Reading this section can create the perception that selling today is a pretty sad state of affairs. And it is, if one plays along with this process.

Low-price providers are the only winners in these cases. The good news is that this process is not as flawless for the buyer as it may appear.

Creating Sameness

So, what's the goal of this cumbersome RFI/RFP process, anyway? It is certainly not designed to allow for provider differentiation, which is troublesome for salespeople. Simply stated, every RFP has the same fundamental goal: to create a commodity out of the product or service they need to acquire. In essence, the buyer is trying to identify the *sameness* in the product being sold. Most RFPs ask questions that do not allow for differentiation, making it easier for the procurement agent to develop an apple-to-apple comparison of the offerings. When the comparison is completed, and all of the products have been leveled to an equal degree of sameness, all the prospect has to do is select the lowest price. A perfect process!

Maybe not. How effective is this process at determining the appropriate vendor? Let's look at a buying scenario to which everyone can relate: supermarkets. An RFP is formulated with the goal of selecting a supermarket. The RFP lists a number of categories on which the buyer will base their selection decision. Questions are asked about various categories such as, "Do you have a produce department that includes bananas, peaches, and grapes?" "Are you open seven days a week?" "Do you have shopping carts?" "Do you accept credit cards?" And more questions of the like.

After analyzing the submissions, the procurement agent creates a comparative grid that looks something like this:

Supermarket RFP Analysis

	Group A	Group B	Group C
Open 7 days a week	YES	YES	YES
Quality Assurance Program	YES	YES	YES
Produce Dept.	YES	YES	YES
Pharmacy	YES	YES	YES
Number of Grocery Carts	800	795	805
Express Checkout Line	YES	YES	YES
Credit Cards Accepted	AMEX, VISA, MC, DISCOVER	AMEX, VISA, MC, DISCOVER	AMEX, VISA, MC, DISCOVER
Multiple Checkout Lines	YES	YES	YES

Based on the matrix, there does not appear to be any significant difference among the three groups. The one area that has a variance is the question about shopping carts. However, the variance is so small for this element that it is insignificant in making a selection decision. The only unanswered question from this grid is price.

The issue is that if the selection decision is made based on the criteria listed in this table, there is a high probability of the wrong supermarket being selected. This comes back to the scoping issue in the RFP process. Quite often, procurement and users have a needs disconnect. This leads to RFP selection criteria being erroneously applied by the procurement agent. As you will see later, this comes about because the agenda of procurement is very different than that of its constituency.

I used the example of a supermarket to illustrate this point because it clearly brings this issue to the forefront, since we all know that there are vast and important differences from supermarket to supermarket. It also shows that the challenge of using the grid approach in buying decisions. The decision of where someone shops has very little to do with the information provided in this grid. Cleanliness, selection, and freshness are just a few of the user requirements that could never be captured through an objective measure of sameness.

On the surface, the RFP appears to measure each supermarket's ability to perform in a wide range of categories. In reality, this RFP will only serve to highlight the low-price provider, which probably will not make the user very happy. By limiting the scope of services the prospect is willing to consider as part of the selection process, the supermarket with the lowest price will win the RFP, since everything else will *seem* to be the same. But we know it's not.

> **Procurement and users often have a communication disconnect resulting in the wrong criteria being applied when selecting a provider.**

Recently, I visited my folks in Marlboro, New Jersey. While there, I needed to pick up some groceries at the new ACME supermarket. Talk about unique! At the entrance, I stumbled upon a mini-Starbucks for a little pick-me-up while shopping. From there, I moved on to the produce section which included something unique as well. Each piece of fruit was in a little slot, like eggs in a carton. No damaged fruit here—each piece was perfect!

The deli section was also a different experience: two counters—one for kosher and one for nonkosher. The differences continued to delight me throughout my shopping experience. The end of the spree was also a unique experience: self-checkout. A pretty satisfying experience!

The supermarket RFP did not identify any of these unique attributes. If I used the RFP to make my decision, I never would have thought to visit this supermarket.

Credit cards can be looked at in much the same way. When I visit a store to make a purchase, I can pull out my American Express, Discover Card, VISA, or MasterCard. All will work to complete the purchase. I hand the cashier the card, they swipe it and return it to me. I walk out of the store with my purchase. At what point does it matter which card was used to complete the transaction? If I have a problem with my purchase, which one of these companies has my back?

I had the opportunity to see this in action. I was on a cruise in the Caribbean when I bought a pair of cowboy boots in Cozumel. When I returned to the ship, I noticed one of the boots had an irreparable rip, but I did not have enough time to return to the store. I called American Express and they removed the charge from my credit card and didn't even want to inspect the boots. How would someone measure that in an RFP or an e-auction?

Dare to Be Different

In a competitive landscape, differentiating yourself becomes more and more challenging. It's the subtle differences that lead one to victory. If one were to look at two ordinary people, few would argue that these people are the same. Or are they? A list can quickly be developed of hundreds of items they have in common.

◆ 2 Hands	◆ 10 Toes	◆ Arteries
◆ 2 Legs	◆ 10 Fingers	◆ Veins
◆ 2 Ears	◆ Mouth	◆ Heart
◆ 2 Eyes	◆ Hair on Head	◆ Stomach
◆ 1 Nose	◆ Brain	◆ 2 Feet

You get the point. But these two ordinary people are very different.

- Hands vary in shape and size
- And feet
- So do legs
- What about hair color?
- And ears
- Eyes vary in color, shape, and size
- And toes
- And fingers
- Gender

Still, there is more on the inside, like:

- Sense of Humor
- Wit
- Passion
- Style
- Intelligence
- Temperament

If all people were the same, friends and dating partners would be easy to find. Just walk outside and pick one. In the everyday world of interaction, people naturally see past the sameness and move right to what is different in them. In the business world, differentiation requires salespeople to help prospects see what is different in their offering when, at surface level, it all looks the same. Today, clients are looking for more than just a simple purchasing relationship. They are looking for support, recommendations, guidance, and ideas.

Consider these two scenarios:

Person 1 walks into a restaurant, reads the menu, and orders a meal. The waiter returns with exactly what was ordered.

Person 2 walks into a restaurant, reads the menu, and orders a meal. The waiter notices the filet mignon was ordered. He quickly advises the diner that the chef has prepared a special vegetable to go with this steak. Further, he recommends a particular wine that was imported specifically to go with this dish. Finally, a dessert is recommended to finish the experience.

Who had the better experience? Both restaurants got the order correctly processed, but which one demonstrated value? Which one showed that they cared? Which showed that they understood their client? Which one made the guest feel special?

"You are all the same." This is what is heard each and every day in the sales world. It's further reinforced through RFPs and e-auctions. Those selling in a takeaway sales environment regularly hear responses of satisfaction with the current provider during prospecting exercises. How does one craft the conversation to bring about discussion of some of the things that are different? My question is: What do you do to provide additional value with your prospects and clients?

Here's the test for this. If one of your prospects wanted to speak with one of your clients as a reference, what value would they say you provide them? Do you take the order and return with the dish? Or do you go above and beyond, and elevate the entire relationship? This is not hypothetical. It is very common for salespeople, when they are perceived also as account managers, to have their value questioned in the reference process.

Reality or a Sales Mirage

It's been a slow sales period for Joe. His pipeline's weak and he is short of his sales goal. Suddenly, out of the blue, an RFP arrives on his desk, promising a huge revenue opportunity. Despite not knowing anyone in this prospect's organization, he dreams of winning the RFP, and spends countless hours preparing this masterpiece. By the time Joe ships off his response, he is convinced that he will be a finalist, and it's a slam-dunk victory. He already has plenty of ideas as to how he will spend his commission check. All of this comes to a grinding halt when a letter is received thanking him for his submission, but informing him that they've selected someone else. He never even got to the table.

What are you to do? The first step is to determine if this process is a formality or if there is a provider change looming. A call is made to the Procurement Agent to understand how and why this was received. The next step is to understand the process for selecting a provider. I encourage you to ask a myriad of questions of the agent in the spirit of determining whether or not it makes sense to participate in this process. Actually, that's the way to begin the conversation.

> "Yes, Mr. Procurement Agent. I've just received this RFP from your company, and I'm trying to determine if it makes sense for us to participate. Can we spend a few minutes discussing it?"

Most agents will agree to speak with the salesperson about the RFP. A strategic plan is needed to handle the dialogue in a way that allows the salesperson to determine if this RFP is worth pursuing.

How did you get on the list to receive this? It's always helpful to find out how this company heard of you. Did they just surf the Net or was this a referral? How many providers have been asked to respond to the RFP?

What is the selection process? Once the RFPs are received, what happens? What are the criteria to become a finalist? Where does price fit into the selection decision?

What is driving this RFP? It is not uncommon for a company to send an RFP for no reason other than that it is a company rule to do so every x number of years. For those, the likelihood of a new provider being selected is low unless there are performance issues. Other times, the RFP is designed for the sole purpose of squeezing the current provider to a lower price point.

Has the company definitively decided to make a change in providers? Sometimes a provider has performed poorly, and the users have asked Procurement to search for another one. The agent won't always share this, but it doesn't hurt to ask.

What is the scope? Rarely are RFPs clear enough to paint the entire picture for a provider to respond with a targeted solution.

Enough questions around the scope can open the door to allow the salesperson to have a conversation with the users. This is the ultimate goal: to get to the users so a relationship can be established. Oftentimes, the agent serves as a gatekeeper and won't allow access to the users. The better-formulated the questions that the agent won't be able to answer (highly technical in nature), the greater the chance of the door being opened to the users.

If the agent refuses to speak with the salesperson, which is rare, there is no point in completing the RFP unless the provider is the low-price purveyor of the industry. I'm amazed at how few salespeople will call the agent and have this conversation. Hey, they don't own my time. I get only a certain number of hours in my day and I cannot waste them on possible sales mirages.

Author, Author!

Not all RFPs are blind ones. Some buying players claim that all purchases in their company must be done through a formal process, which translates to an RFP. Be careful! In many cases, buyers use the RFP process as a means of self-protection. It provides the appearance of having performed due diligence in the purchasing process, which shields the buyer from responsibility in the event a provider doesn't perform as expected. It also spreads out the blame; many RFP decisions are determined by committee, so no single person is fully responsible for the provider's failure. Never underestimate the power of self-protection.

If all is legit and the only way to make this happen is through an RFP, the goal is to become the *author* of the RFP. Few procurement agents know enough about a specific business segment to write an RFP that will meet the user specifications. Many are very general in nature. It's also very frustrating for a salesperson trying to respond to an RFP that was written for a completely different purchasing event.

> **Earned trust and perceived
> uniqueness are the keys to being afforded
> the opportunity to author the RFP.**

The idea here is to design an RFP that brings out the unique attributes of your offering. Some companies have already developed a template RFP that they provide to prospects that require use of one. The RFP is written in such a way that their advantages are brought out and weaknesses hidden. Oftentimes, I will read an RFP and I can tell which of my competitors helped write it. For this offer to be well received, a strong relationship is needed between the prospect and the buying players. It comes down to trust. They need to feel that the salesperson is operating with their best interests in mind. They also need to see the salesperson's offering as unique, and that uniqueness is something they must have.

Recently, I went to one of my favorite men's-clothing stores, Joseph A. Bank. I thought I went to buy a new black-leather jacket since mine had become faded. Since I had received a mailer about a sale, I stopped by to look at their leather jackets. While there, I shared with the manager my concern about the color fading in black-leather jackets. He took the new jacket out of my hand and walked over to the counter. He proceeded to write down the name of a shop that strips and stains leather jackets. The cost for that was a fraction of the price of a new one. Wow! This is a commissioned salesperson who just lost a sale. Not quite. I then spent $300 on a bunch of shirts and I will continue to go to that shop for my men's-clothing needs. What level of trust do you have with your clients? This is one of the themes that will be revisited throughout this book.

If in a salesperson's heart, he feels that his solution is the one that best helps his prospect, he owes it to both himself and his clients to present the RFP tool for use in selecting a provider. To give you an idea of the level of trust that can be developed, I've had salespeople provide an RFP template to companies and they haven't even read the template. How did I know? When they sent it out, they hadn't even changed the part that said, "insert company name here."

If a salesperson's sole objective is to sell something to someone in order to make a big bucket of money, he doesn't belong in sales. Those folks don't have a chance of being successful, as the wrong thing motivates them. If their primary objective is to enhance the lives of their clients, they possess the right core to become a success. If the salesperson is unable to establish a trusting relationship with prospects and clients, he will certainly fail. The importance of trust is everywhere.

A few months ago, I injured my lower back. I went to a chiropractor who I had never used before. While she was treating me, she kept "selling" me on the benefits of chiropractics. Ironically, I've used chiropractic care before, and am a believer in its techniques. Yet, she kept selling me. It got to a point whereby I felt she cared more about a continued revenue stream than my health. I quickly found someone else to treat me.

Trust is a major factor in determining if a salesperson will have the opportunity to craft the RFP for a prospect. The right mindset for the salesperson will help to ensure that happens.

CHAPTER 6
Dare to Be Different!

"A ship is safe in harbor, but that's not what ships are for."
—William Shedd

The Toughest Competitor to Defeat

Sales is very competitive. You already knew that. But who is the competition? I'd argue that there are always two types of competitors who are faced in every buying process, but they are defeated in two different ways. When I ask salespeople to identify their competition, they quickly recite a laundry list of providers who offer similar products and services to their own. Most of them miss the big one, the most powerful one. Ironically, the one they miss is the one killing their deals more than any of the providers on their list. This competitor is a *Latin powerhouse* who has a stronghold on the account. This competitor is in the mind of every one of the buying players. He is in their minds long after you leave. Few prepare adequately to battle him. He is ruthless. Buyers love him because he makes their decision easy and offers great advantages. Few can beat him, for he has key powers that can stop the deal in its tracks. His name is "STATUS QUO."

Let's look at an abstract example of just how powerful status quo can be:

Two coworkers, Jamie and Steven, visit their local cafeteria for lunch.

"Everything looks so good! I'm *famished*! I didn't get to eat breakfast this morning," gushes Jamie.

Steven, on the other hand, says, "Lots of options, but I don't see anything that tickles my fancy. I'm not that hungry anyway. I had a big breakfast and am going out for dinner tonight. I'm not going to get anything."

On the way back to the office, Jamie begins eating right in the elevator.

A surprised Steven exclaims, "My goodness! You can't wait five minutes to get back to the office?"

"I can't," replies Jamie between mouthfuls, "I'm starving! If I don't eat something now, I feel like I'll pass out."

Imagine Jamie and Steven are prospects. They represent the opposite ends of the buying spectrum. Jamie is *starving*. She needs to eat; she *has* to eat. She is uncomfortable because she hasn't eaten. She must eat, and quickly. She has but one question in her mind: What is she going to eat?

In a buying process, Jamie is described as a buying player who is motivated to make a change; the only question in her mind is to whom. Her present situation is intolerable and change is critical. She can articulate exactly why her situation is intolerable and what will happen if a change is not made, and made quickly.

On the other hand, Steven would probably eat if something tickled his fancy. He doesn't necessarily know what that is. He's not looking for food, but he will certainly accompany a coworker who is hungry.

Steven represents the buying player that is comfortable with the current provider, or at least not uncomfortable enough to pursue something different. The salesperson's role is to find a way to motivate *Steven* to take action. Prospect motivation is a challenge that, without proper preparation, will open the door for status quo to "win" the business. The challenge is that "Steven" prospects will always be inclined to award the business to status quo over any other option.

"Jamie" prospects are handled very differently from "Steven" prospects. Most salespeople can manage the Jamie prospects well as they probably have competitive intelligence, like marketing slicks and proposals. They've seen their competitor's Web sites and have heard anecdotes from other clients and prospects about the competition. From fighting in the trenches, they have an idea of the competition's approach to handling pricing. Quite frankly, salespeople usually know their competitor's tricks. I'm willing to wager that some of you can discuss your competitor's strategy and offering better than your own. However, a hidden danger in the buying process is that the buyer can quickly change from a Jamie to a Steven if care is not exercised. If the provider selection process is too cumbersome to make a change, the fire in Jamie's stomach will be quickly extinguished. Now the salesperson has to deal with Steven.

> ## Status quo is always a strong option for buyers.

The first step in understanding status quo is the acceptance that he always has an offer on the buyer's table. Prospects always reserve the right to keep things as they are. It's always an option. For many buyers, it is the safest option. As salespeople, acknowledging that status quo exists and setting their sights on defeating him is a key step. What's interesting about analyzing the impact of status quo is that he is the number-one killer of the opportunity pipeline, but few focus their efforts on understanding and defeating him.

Getting inside a prospect's mind is the next step to defeating status quo. Before selecting a new provider, a buyer first decides to pursue a change. If the salesperson is successful at creating that motivation, the next step is for the buyer to select a provider from the masses. The eagle salespeople focus their sales approach using this same two-step process.

But how committed is the prospect to making a change? They'd best be strong reasons, as status quo has four advantages that no salesperson *ever* has working for them.

Fear of Change: Ever heard the old expression, "The devil you know is better than the devil you don't?" This kind of reasoning gives a buyer pause, as he wonders if this solution will really be better than the existing one. Most people don't get excited about change. Change is very scary for people. The more the provider's product or service changes the way someone does something, the more challenging the adoption of change will be for the buyer. Status quo makes the buyer wonder if the benefits discussed are real or merely a mirage. Can this new solution really be that much better than the way things are today? He wonders if he will truly save the 30 percent that has been presented to him by the other provider.

While many providers position themselves as *revolutionizing the workplace* as a strategy to win, they just may be scaring their prospects to death. It's something to monitor. The approach to managing the fear of change varies based on the individual buying player and their business culture.

A great example of how status quo leverages fear of change is in the world of information technology (IT). Every company is either integrating or migrating to new technology. The question in the minds of the IT buying player is when is the right time to add or change technology. They know that today's product becomes outdated tomorrow. They worry about investing in technology that becomes outdated. How can you help a buying player work through this?

One way is to use a driving metaphor. Imagine driving down the on-ramp of a major highway. The driver gets to the end of the ramp and is faced with a glut of speeding cars. The driver has two choices. Wait for all of the cars to stop so he can proceed. Or the more realistic solution is to accelerate and proceed to the destination. The IT world works in much the same way. Technology innovation will never stop. Thus, the choice is to invest knowing that and get the efficiency gains afforded with the new solution or remain stagnant. The real question is does this technology solution solve the business problem at hand? In essence, the discussion focus moves from fear of change to the business problem(s) solved by an infusion of new technology.

Fear of Blame: Will I be fired, demoted, or embarrassed if the new solution backfires? In contrast to the fear of change, the individual who makes the buying decision is accountable for better or worse. Status quo regularly reminds the buyer of this fact and focuses on the worst-case scenario. Not all buying players are willing to fight the fight, especially if they work in a culture that has a low tolerance for mistakes.

I've seen a number of deals evaporate because the buying player focused her management on how poorly their current provider performed. She hadn't selected that provider; she inherited the relationship. However, if she selected someone new, this responsibility would fall on her. Ultimately, she decided that it was better for her to complain about what she inherited instead of making a change.

These first two fears can paralyze buyers and end the pursuit of a provider change very quickly. Unfortunately, falling prey to these fears is very embarrassing for the buyer. When status quo wins using those competitive advantages, a call will not come from the prospect telling the salesperson that they are afraid of the repercussions of making a provider change. Buyers tend to just disappear when their fear keeps them beholden to status quo. When voice and e-mail messages go unreturned, that is a good sign that the deal has been lost to status quo. There are two additional advantages that status quo presents: priority and lack of time.

Priority: Status quo reminds the buyer that there are bigger priorities than this one. Why this one now? Why not leave this alone for a while. Most of the buying players encountered are not financially compensated for improving the company for which they work. They are paid a salary, that's it. So why would they sign up for more work? How does this benefit them personally?

By the way, who is going to champion this and deal with the work associated with implementing a new provider? When status quo wins based on the "priority" advantage, the buyer will say that resources to make a change are unavailable or that other priorities have moved to the forefront. They will sound distant when they are a little embarrassed for having looked at a change in the first place.

To defeat status quo, the salesperson facilitates a discussion with the buying player to offset those competitive advantages. Being proactive is key because if status quo brings these points to light first, he wins. This can be accomplished by asking questions around those competitive advantages.

With status quo defeated, the next step is to battle the other providers. Remembering the goal of the buyer is to level the playing field to create a sameness environment; the mission is to execute a strategy that focuses the buyer's attention on the provider's area of differentiation.

I know many salespeople are very concerned about pricing. After all, no one pays more for the same thing. Or do they? I'll bet many of you already spend 700 percent more for the same product. The variance is where you buy it. Don't believe me? Look at this...

"Where's the Beef?"

After a frustrating morning of cold-calling prospects, David, hungry for a burger, heads to the local McDonalds. Thinking,

"There's nothing like a double cheeseburger for $0.99 to really hit the spot," he places his order at the counter and, within minutes, is devouring his lunch.

Later that day, his friend Sharon invites him to dinner at their favorite local restaurant. Still craving red meat, he opens the menu in search of another burger. Eureka! There it is: another double cheeseburger. Without a thought for the $7.99 price tag, he orders his second double cheeseburger of the day.

While they ate, David begins to recount his day. Gloomy and exhausted, he vents his frustrations:

"I've got to get a new job. My $0.99 double cheeseburger was the highlight of my day. Every prospect I call bases their decision upon price. That's the way they all see it: if you aren't the low-price purveyor, you lose. Even though my company's service includes so much more bang for the buck, all they see is that my service costs 10 percent more than that of my closest competitor, end of story."

Sharon replies, "So, your solution is more robust than your competitor's, but your prospects just don't see it? It sounds to me like they're asking, 'Where's the beef?' Let me ask you a simple question: Would you pay 10 percent more if you thought the service was the same?"

"Of course not," David confesses.

Sharon then asks, "How about one-percent more?"

"Again, no," replies David.

Sharon then observes, "Well, you had no problem ordering that cheeseburger for 700 percent more than the one you had for lunch. Unless, of course, you think *I'm* buying."

David counters, "It's not the same."

"No?" asks Sharon. "It's a double cheeseburger, two all-beef-patty cheeseburgers with a pickle, lettuce, tomato, and ketchup on a roll. Where's the difference?"

"There are a bunch of differences!" argues David. "A waiter brought this to me while I sat comfortably at the table. The restaurant has a quiet ambiance. The burger was served on a plate instead of in a paper wrapper, and the bun was a kaiser roll."

Sharon then exclaims, "Aha! A 700-percent increase for a kaiser roll! What a bargain!"

"But it's more than that," David explains. "You aren't just paying for the cheeseburger. You're paying for the whole experience: a professional chef in the kitchen, a comfortable chair, and a linen napkin. All of these things have associated costs, but they also add value."

Sharon counters, "So, you can easily justify 700 percent, but you can't get your prospects to justify 10 percent. I guess you have two choices here: Find a way to communicate the difference to justify the cost to your customers, or—"

"Or, I'll be the one serving cheeseburgers, I get it," David admits.

Commodity

Since the buyer's goal is to create commodity when they buy, a strategy is needed to combat that approach. That said, it's not unusual to feel insulted at having your offering referred to as a "commodity," or to believe this label should be avoided at all costs. Typically, the morning a salesperson wakes up thinking that their offering has become just another commodity is the day they start e-mailing out resumes (assuming that they are not the low-price provider).

Most salespeople are on a quest to ensure that their company's offering never becomes perceived as a commodity. But commodity is a valuable trait of any marketplace. Who says that commodity is all bad?

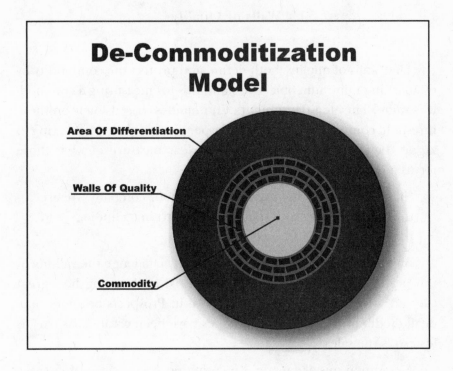

From one perspective, being viewed as a commodity is a poor reflection of the offering. It reduces the sale to one issue: price. "Why buy gadget A for $2 when I can purchase gadget B for $1?" That seems like a valid perspective, but only until a closer look is taken at what it really means to be a commodity.

A more precise view is that commodity translates to baseline credibility. Commodity represents the standard for all products or services within a class. Prospects won't spend more for a product based on commodity, but commodity is useful because it does set a minimum benchmark for a buyer's expectations. To help ensure the prospect's view extends beyond the basic commodity aspects of the provider, the strategy is to eliminate from consideration those providers who do not meet that standard.

Walls of Quality

The "walls of quality" both define and protect the commodity by establishing minimum objective standards for measuring a commodity's value. They limit argument of uniqueness based solely on these threshold commodity aspects. As salespeople, many err when trying to argue "better" and "best," without a clear measure of what those terms mean to a buyer.

> "Let me tell you why you should select our company. We are the market leader, with the state of the art in technology, and the best service in the industry."

Buyers don't buy it! The walls of quality challenge the validity of this argument, but many salespeople insist on boasting how great they are when there is no way to prove it. Prospects become tone-deaf; credibility is lost and trust issues have been created. As trust is lost, so is the sale.

A common mistake made is focusing on *better* instead of *different*. I don't recall ever hearing a salesperson describe their company's technology as mediocre or their service as pretty good. It never happens! However, buyers continue to hear that "best" sales mantra.

> **The primary goal of a buyer is to pay the lowest price that matches his needs and desires.**

To further make this point, let's consider two drivers, both with clean driving records. So, which driver is *better*? The answer is that driving records don't provide the answer. One may be a great driver and the other, terrible, but the walls of quality, e.g., their driving records, can't help draw a distinction between the two if *neither* had any tickets or accidents. Since the walls of quality are built upon driving records as a benchmark of driving proficiency, these drivers' abilities are perceived as equal regardless of the reality. Just ask the car-insurance companies.

The real lesson is that the walls of quality set the bottom benchmark, and can eliminate those who cannot rise above it.

In another example, it is difficult to make the argument that one Certified Public Accountant (CPA) is better than another CPA. The argument doesn't fly because a CPA certification is perceived as a minimum benchmark of quality for accountants. Building up the walls of quality makes sense when a CPA competes against a non-CPA accountant. However, it is highly unlikely for one CPA to argue that they are a better CPA than another.

Nevertheless, the prospect hasn't agreed to buy from a particular provider yet, but the salesperson has potentially eliminated the first class of competitors (after status quo), or at least helped their prospect to see their shortcomings. A connection, trust, has been developed—the crucial first step in any buying process—and building walls of quality around the basic commodity made that possible. The commodity baseline eliminated a second level of competition, as those who couldn't meet the basic standard were also eliminated.

The next step is to bring out the area of differentiation. What makes this provider unique, and why will a prospect care about this uniqueness?

Area of Differentiation

"If you nail two things together that have never been nailed together before, someone will buy it!" This simple expression from comedian George Carlin truly describes how people buy. To see this truism at work, take a stroll through an arts-and-crafts show. Artists glue together five nails and elbow macaroni, name it "Joy Frolicking in Sunshine," and price the work at thirty bucks. If someone finds it uniquely charming and wants to buy it, they are in a pretty weak bargaining position. How could they not be? No one else is offering such a product, which means they pay the craftsman's price to get what they want. Differentiation is based on a fundamental principle: Uniqueness allows providers to sell at their asking price.

There is a common misconception in sales that when a deal is lost it is because the buyer made the purchasing decision primarily based upon price. This mantra may make some feel better, but not the eagle salespeople! However, if everyone based their buying decision solely on price, everyone would drive Hyundais! Don't get me wrong. There are some people who only look at price. Most people will pay the price that gets them the solution that most closely meets their needs and desires.

> # No one pays more for something they perceive as the same.

Make no mistake, people will *not* pay a higher price to get what they perceive as sameness. When a sale is lost on price, what is really heard is that the value portrayed did not justify the price delta. Buyers don't make it easy to be different. They are constantly trying to lump all providers into a sameness bucket so they can perform what is commonly referred to as an apple-to-apple comparison, the product resulting from the RFP. As you saw before, the only winner in that type of comparison is low price, unless the playing field is changed.

The key is to lead the prospect to the provider's "area of differentiation." This term refers to the unique attributes that are offered beyond commodity. These attributes help to justify a higher price in a prospect's mind. Since buyers cannot be convinced of better quality in a commodity, the strategy is to help the prospect see the solution as unique. The good news is that people are willing to pay more if they believe they have found uniqueness.

It is not an easy task to find the area of differentiation in a mature (commodity) marketplace. This is accomplished by analyzing what the provider, as a whole, offers as a solution to a client's problems. The concern is that if the area of differentiation is not found or, more importantly, can't be communicated effectively to a prospect, the only remaining decision point for buyers is price.

Case Study: The Information-Technology Training Industry

To ensure client satisfaction with their technology products, software companies develop training programs to educate users on their products. The fundamental reason they do this is that if client satisfaction with their product is high, the client will buy more software from them.

To deliver this training, most software companies develop a "training channel" to deliver training through partner companies rather than provide the training themselves. Even though these partner companies are independently owned, the software manufacturers set the rules. They develop and write the courseware, certify the instructors, and set the standards for the PCs and servers in the classrooms. The goal of the software manufacturer is to create a "vanilla" program that allows them to tell their clients to go to any of their partners for a great training experience. In essence, the software companies have intentionally created a "commodity." The commodity sets a baseline for them, which helps them with their clients. In the end, however, it created a challenge for their channel partners.

Interestingly, the one area that most software companies did not address for their partners was price. The partners usually sold courses at whatever the market would bear. Back to an earlier point, who is going to pay more for one provider over another when there is a perception of sameness? Based on the software company's approach, the customer was guaranteed to have the software company's curriculum, a software-company certified instructor, and the same equipment in the classroom, regardless of which partner delivered the training class. In essence, the education itself became the commodity.

Salespeople for the various partner companies continually tried to make the argument that their course delivery was "better," but the "walls of quality" did not allow it. Buyers would not accept the arguments that one provider's instructors were better than another, or that one's curriculum was superior because the walls of quality had already set a standard in the industry that all partner training centers were alike. This led to a dramatic drop in the price for these courses as more training centers were added to the channel.

However, one provider saw a different picture. As painful as it was, this company gave into the clients, in principle, that its classes were not necessarily better than any other provider's. At least, they accepted that they could not prove it to a prospect. Instead, the company saw that the area of differentiation literally was outside the walls—the walls of the classroom, that is—and came up with a unique approach. They looked at the challenges facing their clientele. This training company realized that the main difficulty was selling to information-technology management. These managers had two particular challenges: hiring and retaining employees in the face of a tremendous shortage of qualified talent, and finding time to procure training for their employees. These IT managers had a four-page job description and procuring training for their people was not high on their duty list. There was a link between these two challenges: Many studies cited a lack of training as a main reason people left to pursue new opportunities. This exposed a significant opportunity for the training company to impact its client's business. These IT managers had no time to deal with what their employees viewed as important, which caused employees to look elsewhere for jobs, and forced the IT managers to find new talent to replace the outgoing talent.

This training company established a strategy to make the process of procuring training easier for its clients. Actually, the first step was to recognize that it had two clients, the IT manager and the class attendee. This allowed them to make a fundamental shift in how they approached their sales strategy. Price quickly became a non-issue because the packaging was unique and the prospects were willing to pay more for the added value. While this training provider's competitors continued to argue that their trainers were better, this company was winning mega deals at 20–30 percent higher margins.

"You've Got the Right One, Baby"

In another example of differentiation, on March 25, 2002, an article appeared in *The Wall Street Journal* to which most people probably paid little attention. The article titled, "Pepsi to Bump Coke as Cola of Choice on United Airlines," just seemed like just another win in the fairy tale "Cola Wars." Or was it? Note the date of the announcement. A mere six months after the 9/11 tragedy, someone was able to put together "a soda deal" with an airline. This was a time when most of us would have thought that airlines were exclusively focused on enhancing their security programs.

One can only guess that this was not a failed "taste test" for Coca-Cola. The Pepsi deal is a five-year arrangement which ends a decades long relationship with Coke to be the cola of choice on United Airlines. What is unique about this is that Pepsi and United will be involved in joint marketing and promotional programs designed to enhance each other's revenue. Very creative!

The NOS Wars

In the early 1990s, Novell owned about 70 percent of the networking-operating-system (NOS) market with their Netware product. However, Microsoft quickly saw this opportunity as one of their next horizons. In early '90s, they launched WindowsNT as their competitive product. As most of you know, Microsoft never enters a market unless they are going to dominate it. They invested millions in sales and marketing. Seemingly overnight, they took market share away from Novell. By the mid '90s, Novell had the largest-installed base of these NOS, but Microsoft was the fastest-growing company. By the late '90s, Microsoft had achieved its objective and had become both the largest provider and the quickest to expand in this time period.

This phenomenon happens every day. However, this story has a twist. In the early and mid-90s, if you asked most IT professionals their choice of NOS, they would give you a surprising answer: Novell Netware. They felt Netware was more stable and reliable. They felt that WindowsNT had numerous design flaws in the early days. In essence, Microsoft crushed Novell with a seemingly inferior product. They accomplished this by becoming a sales-and-marketing machine.

There are countless other examples of successes and failures in differentiating. Regardless of how different the provider may be, the inability to articulate it may negate the differentiation. I introduce to you: the sound-byte.

CHAPTER 7
Wow! Listen to That!

"To effectively communicate, we must realize that we are all different
in the way we perceive the world and use this understanding
as a guide to our communication with others."
—Anthony Robbins

Sounding Different

Messaging is one of the most daunting tasks facing business professionals. From the CEO to the salesperson, articulating a unique story in a short, yet effective, few moments is a most challenging task. However, if the message can't be clearly and quickly articulated, prospects will never be motivated to consider doing business with the provider. Yes, differentiation is important, but it doesn't really matter if it cannot be communicated in a meaningful way. When I've talked to salespeople about differentiation, rarely have I found salespeople that can articulate it in a way that is clear and powerful. That's where many fall down. Differentiation is not something that is a feature or benefit of a product or service. It's an overall message. The *sound-byte* is the foundation for that message. This is not to be confused with an elevator story, which is a brief sales pitch. Elevator stories lack structure, formalized content, or consistent approach. They also lack "oomph." Needless to say, I'm not a fan of the basic concept. The sound-byte becomes the foundation for a variety of elements within a salesperson's Sales Architecture. Segments of it are used at varying phases of the buying process such as a telephonic introduction, a written introduction, a kickoff to a needs analysis meeting, etc.

So, let's get started on putting yours together. For starters, we'll set a baseline that this is going to be a powerful, three-minute, compelling story that answers why someone should do business with you and your firm. Rest assured, I'm not suggesting that someone will listen to a three-minute soliloquy. It will never be recited to a prospect, but it will serve a variety of purposes. Think of this in the same way that a movie is developed. Countless hours of film are recorded, only to use 90 minutes for the film. Same goes here. The plan is to whittle this down to the most effective message. At the other end of the spectrum, while three minutes seems like a long time, it's surprising how quickly the time goes when you first start to put this together. When I conduct workshop sessions on sound-byte formulation, salespeople think they are approaching three minutes when they are already over five minutes. For starters, keep the limit to three minutes in this initial development phase of the sound-byte.

> **Being unique is important, but it loses all importance if it cannot be clearly articulated in a meaningful way.**

Based on an individual's particular selling style (remember, I don't provide scripts), a number of elements of the sound-byte are customized. The order of those elements is less important than telling the story with a logical flow. It is important to note that while one may be proud of their position in the marketplace, a sound-byte that focuses only on features (i.e., product and service descriptors) will not excite the audience.

The Showstopper

"Holy cow! What did he just say? I've never heard that before." Wouldn't sales be great if every prospect responded this way? It can be done if key differentiating techniques called "showstoppers" are utilized.

The goal is to have the audience on the edge of their seat. Their total, undivided attention is needed. With this in mind, the "showstopper" concept is used to introduce the sound-byte. To accomplish this, a brief, powerful opening statement that will clearly get the attention of the audience is necessary.

> **Buyers buy from salespeople that appear to have the complete support of their organization's resources.**

Most salespeople elect to start with a historical soliloquy. Yawn! This approach puts the audience to sleep. Everyone does that. They've heard it all before. Who cares that you opened in 1980 and are based in Chicago? Should that mean something to them? Quite frankly, with that approach, the airfare can be saved with a CD-ROM sent to the prospect with the provider's corporate overview. What buying players want to hear immediately is what makes this provider *special*.

"The showstopper" is the opening statement designed to grab the crowd. It is a powerful introductory statement that separates this provider from all of his potential competitors, including status quo. It is meant to be colorful, yet truly position-unique.

One approach to introduce the "showstopper" might be this:

"I'm sure many of you have spoken with other providers who offer similar services and have one simple question in mind: What makes us different from all of the other providers? Simply put, our clients come to us for the following reason(s)..."

The reasons need to be better than, "because we have the best service, yada, yada, yada." Powerful! Hard-hitting! This opening paves the way for an emphatic expression of what is different. One that I've seen used effectively in some industries is:

"We don't have any customers."

Seems like a ridiculous statement. Or is it? If one were to look up the word "customer" in Webster's Dictionary, a simple definition would be found: "One who buys goods or services." However, what if you use a different word, one that is commonly used as a synonym: "client"?

According to Webster's, the definition of a client is: "One who depends on the protection of another." Imagine representing to a buying player this subtlety as a way of sounding different from all of the other salespeople who are in pursuit of their business. Granted, this can only be used as a differentiator if the provider truly manages their business in that way. For example, if a salesperson were selling security-guard services, this is a very powerful statement. Their clients are looking for protection. They would be hard-pressed to argue that their security guards are bigger or tougher than the competition's.

The rest of the sound-byte is composed of support statements around the "showstopper." These support statements are best provided through case studies-stories of how the provider has helped specific clients. Most salespeople will list, in a table-of-contents fashion, all of the wonderful things their company can do. This is rarely effective. Buyers love case studies! They build confidence and credibility.

> **Sharing client success stories is a powerful way to communicate corporate capabilities.**

The key for the salesperson is to have an arsenal of these anecdotes that can be plugged in and played based on the buyer's circumstances. The more relevant the case study, the more powerful the sound-byte. For purposes of this exercise, formulate four strong case studies that are brief and powerful. For example, describe a problem, or a series of problems, that a client experienced prior to working with your organization. Next, summarize how you creatively solved the problem and discuss the client's results in using the solution:

> "ABC company is a great example of how we partner with our clients. In working with their former provider, they experienced constant overcharging due to erroneous billing. Knowing this, we implemented their program using our specialized billing system. They've been with us for three years, no billing errors. They've shared with us that this has saved them over $10,000 per year in saved accounts-payable time."

Many salespeople forget the last component of this message. It is critical to include the benefits the client received in tangible expressions as listed in the example. If the buying players heard nothing else, they heard XYX Corporation improved their bottom line by working with you. Quite often, buying players typically write down client names and keywords. This goes a long way toward establishing credibility.

In addition, it is important that the overview touches on all of the main advantages of the provider's offerings and the reasons why clients found them to be beneficial. Being thorough is key because the purpose of the meeting may be to discuss one offering, while there may be a stronger interest in another. Be on the lookout for the unexpected sale!

Company History

As stated earlier, the goal is not to win an Emmy Award for most-thorough presentation of the history of the company. However, relevant facts from a buyer's perspective are helpful. The story of how the company came into existence can be a useful tool for building credibility. The following basic information may be appropriate elements as well. A word of caution: It may be more effective to present the company by describing its present makeup, and then tell the historical, chronological story. Dates and metrics may be key points of mention.

One of the key areas important to mention when discussing company value is how the provider measures quality. Buyers are very focused on buying quality for their dollar. The main responsibility of purchasing managers is identifying quality providers who match to their constituency's needs. However, everyone has his or her own definition of quality. I had the privilege of attending procurement training a few years ago. It was the best sales-training experience I have ever experienced. This training taught procurement agents how to buy. Quite frankly, I felt like a spy in this course, but it was great. There is an exam that many purchasing folks take called the CPM (Certified Purchasing Manager) exam. The curriculum is designed to train buyers on how to analyze a provider's quality through:

- ◆ Tangible examples of management commitment
- ◆ Development of employees
- ◆ Use of metrics to measure and monitor the operation
- ◆ Use of client feedback to improve operations

Tying these into the sound-byte is sure to hit the right buttons with the buying community.

Personal Value

Personal value is one of the most overlooked advantages that eagle salespeople have in their back pocket. "If you select our firm, you get me." Each of you has value beyond what your companies bring to bear. The key is for the buyer to see that value in you as you represent your firm. Buyers are always asking themselves why they should buy from you. Credibility is very important to them as they look at you as their primary support vehicle. To develop this element of the sound-byte, look at your personal history to see what can be extrapolated to create value for a buying player.

For example, if you worked for the same company for twelve years, you could talk about why you have stayed with the company at a time when employment tenure is at an all-time low. In addition, you could discuss what you have learned from implementing solutions to your own clientele. As a new salesperson, you could talk about what attracted you to join the organization. This could help you relate well to a prospect, as they would be seeing the situation from a similar perspective.

If a salesperson were new to an industry, but was an account manager for five years in another one, they could talk about what they learned from that experience, such as the importance of service. They could then tie-in that experience to share with the prospect, as this is how they will support the buyer after the sale is made. Many buyers fear the old "sell and go." That's when the salesperson closes the deal and disappears. The more confidence the salesperson can build regarding the support he will provide, the more powerful the message.

Need another way to differentiate yourself? How about creating a "client neighborhood?" This is an e-mail group that you use to share interesting information with prospects and clients. Today, it is an industry-related article. Next week, it is an update on a regulatory change affecting your clientele. The idea is that this is an easy way to touch your buying players on a regular basis and create value. Later when I get into references, think about the impact of a client telling a prospect how you support them.

Audience

Knowing the audience and crafting a sound-byte that speaks to them requires a review of the different types of people encountered in the buying process. By doing homework on this element, the eagle salesperson can take advantage of the opportunity to share some of the challenges learned from working with other organizations.

An example of this component for a CFO is:

"We typically work with the CFO of an organization on projects like this. We've found CFOs are typically focused on three areas: outsourcing, vendor consolidation, and budget management. Our programs are designed to address those areas with minimal disruption to the company."

It's always interesting to watch a buying player's face when one of these challenges strikes a nerve. They will lean forward in their seat, perhaps grin and nod, and then start asking a ton of questions to better understand how the solution is delivered. Later in the book, an overall analysis of buying players is conducted that will help to strengthen this component.

An Uzi to Kill a Fly?

After all of that content on the importance of delivering a complete picture of capabilities, I'm going to give you a headache, not any headache, "an Excedrin headache." Does that expression sound vaguely familiar? If you recall, this pain-reliever was marketed as having superior strength over its competition. However, sales did not take off with this campaign as the manufacturer had hoped. After marketing research, the manufacturer found that consumers continued to use their regular pain-reliever for regular pain. They only used Excedrin for their "Excedrin-type" headaches.

As the salesperson describes the possibilities, the impression created of being too big or powerful for the necessary solution can cause concern. It could create the impression that your solution is too broad (i.e., expensive) for the problem being experienced.

Language

Language can serve to differentiate as well, for example, here are three seemingly interchangeable words: "vendor," "provider," and "partner." However, each of these has a unique definition.

"Vendor" has a short, simple definition. It is simply defined by Webster's as "one who sells." In the Spanish language, the word "vender" simply means, "to sell." No additional value is associated with this expression. It infers a brief relationship highlighted with a quick transaction. When I think of a vendor, I think of a one-time buying situation where no relationship is ever established.

When one analyzes the word "provider," a very different perspective is depicted: "to fill sufficiently, satisfy, supply a need." These two words have very little in common, but are used by both buyers and salespeople all the time. The inference from "provider" is a much more in-depth understanding of a buyer's problems. How else could one satisfy a need?

To take this one step further, a look at the word "partner" shows a third different definition: "one who is united or associated with another or others in an activity or sphere of common interest." In contrast to "vendor" and "provider," this is a very different meaning. The inference of "partner" is that the relationship is mutually beneficial and a close bond is developed.

That said, many salespeople use the term "partner" without truly understanding the definition. It is a sales buzzword that has become commodity in the minds of buyers. If a salesperson is going to use any of those terms (particularly provider and partner), the synergy needs to be clearly explained.

Another powerful way to differentiate with language is with the perspective of price versus cost. Price is simply the amount of an invoice for a product or service. The cost is the overall impact that the product or service has on the organization. Procurement agents are often taught the difference, but not salespeople. A term often heard is "total cost of ownership," (TCO).

Let's consider the following scenario.

Kirtz Industries is in the process of procuring cleaning services for its offices. The Newman Cleaning Company is offering a price of $300 per cleaning. However, The Baby Cleaning Company is offering a price of $250. Who should get the business? After all, it's just cleaning services, or is it?

After further analysis, it turns out that The Baby Cleaning Company is not bonded (insurance protection from loss), does not have a team supervisor onsite to manage the cleaners, and uses cheap cleaning materials.

In comparison, The Newman Cleaning Company is bonded, includes an onsite supervisor for the cleaners in their price, and uses high-grade cleaning materials. While it will cost $50 more per cleaning to use Newman, Kirtz Industries will not need to have their own supervisory personnel at the office to manage the cleaning staff, a significant savings.

The argument of better materials is not a strong differentiator by itself. However, the bonding and management issues are significant. Now, it's decision time.

If the decision is made on price, Baby Cleaning Company gets the business—$50 savings.

If the decision is made on cost, Newman Cleaning Company gets the business—$50 savings.

The sales job is to guide the buying decision so the buying players see this difference.

Humor

The power of laughter is immeasurable in sales. Countless books have referenced this as a great way to develop rapport. An easy example of this is to look at your own background. If you've been in a particular industry for a long time, you can say, "I've been doing this since Columbus got off the boat." On of my longtime salespeople refers to herself as being in the industry since dirt. This expression builds rapport and credibility in one fell swoop. Look for key places in the sound-byte to interject these humorous comments, as it will help create a bond.

Sound-byte Checklist

1. Does the "showstopper" communicate a strong differentiated message? Is it clear?

2. Does the rest of the sound-byte support the "showstopper?"

3. Is the sequence of the story logical and easy to follow?

4. Does the sound-byte incorporate all that the provider can bring to bear?

5. Is it told in the buyer's language versus industry jargon?

6. Can the story be told with passion that will excite a buyer?

7. Are case studies included that show the client's results?

8. Does the capability story match the prospect's needs?

9. Is the story of my company exciting or does it sound like someone reading a history textbook?

10. Has personal value been shared?

11. How much humor has been incorporated into the story?

12. Did the end remind the audience of the showstopper?

Putting It All Together

The old joke about how you get to Carnegie Hall, "practice, practice, practice." holds very true here. At the beginning of this section, I referenced that this yields a three-minute sound-byte which will never be used in that fashion. Once this is down to three minutes, find a colleague from whom you can receive some coaching. Deliver the sound-byte to your colleague, and ask the following:

♦ Did the showstopper get your attention?

♦ What message did you receive?

♦ What do you recall?

♦ What sounded different?

♦ What was effective? Why was it effective?

♦ What didn't make sense? What would have been better?

Once you do that, trim the sound-byte down to 2.5 minutes and perform the same exercise. Keep doing that until you have a 30-second message that is powerful! That becomes your introductory piece on the phone for prospects. An extrapolation is used for an e-mail introduction, and an introduction to a corporate presentation, etc.

As you go through this, keep asking yourself the following:

◆ Can I say more with fewer words/sentences?

◆ Does this section provide value to the listener?

◆ Have I used their language or my industry's language?

◆ How am I making myself unique?

CHAPTER 8
Navigating Through the Account

"If we're growing, we're always going to be out of our comfort zone."
—John Maxwell, American Author

Selling Mom and Dad

Ever been to a "Murder Mystery" event? Typically, there is a room of about fifty people who are tasked with solving a murder. All fifty people are suspects. Two hours are given to solve the crime, starting with very few, if any, clues. Two hours, that's it. After two hours, the event is over. Was it the man with the blue hat? Or maybe the woman in the green dress? No one knows who did it, but the group knows that the killer is among that group of fifty players. Was there an accomplice? Could be. The task is to figure all of that out in two hours flat.

> **Effective facilitation of the buying process requires the salesperson to recognize the various buying player roles.**

Selling in a complex environment is much the same. It requires engagement of a number of different players in the buying process.

Their role, agenda, and needs are unknown. Yet, there is a task of navigating through this investigation much like the "whodunit" sleuth. Who makes the buying decision? Who is going to kill the deal? Who likes the competitor's solution? Who can help the win? These are just a sampling of the questions that eagle salespeople ask themselves when they set forth on this quest. This section will provide a roadmap to assist with the navigation through an organization to identify the various roles that people play in the buying process.

For starters, all of the people encountered along the way are players in the buying process. Thus, they are called "buying players." You have probably noticed that I have been using this term throughout the book. These players may play multiple roles in the buying process. Affecting the roles that these people play in the buying process are company culture, nature of the product, price, and a hundred other factors.

The concept of understanding buying players is best understood when looking at the parent/child relationship. As a child, it was fairly easy to manage the process of getting what you wanted. First, it was known that the decision was going to be made by one and/or two people...Mom and/or Dad. Second, a relationship existed allowing for predicting each one's reaction to a given situation. This was developed over years of asking for various things and gauging the reaction of each of them based on the nature of the request.

As a youngster, there was no strategy. You wanted what you wanted, when you wanted it. If you didn't get it, you may have pouted, screamed, or cried. Some may have done all three. You saw how your parents responded. You saw who the softy was. Oftentimes, one of the parents was typically softer than the other.

This created a learning process. You saw what affected decisions with each of them. Maybe Dad gave in just to stop the crying. Perhaps Mom gave in because she didn't want to be embarrassed at the mall. The key was that all the while, you were learning about how decisions were made, and most importantly, you were receiving an education on how to get decisions made in your favor.

Age allowed for the use of that particular strategy. Screaming and pouting became no longer weapons in the arsenal. Other tactics to positively affect the decision replaced them. For example, knowing that both Mom and Dad had to approve spending in excess of your allowance created one strategy. Reason for, and amount of, spending resulted in a different strategy being deployed.

As maturity took place, it became easier and easier figure out which one to go to first to *get them on your side* based on how much you were asking for and what you wanted to buy. As a result, the older you got, your success improved because you had a unique strategy. When a new bike was desired, you knew whom to ask first and how to engage him or her. The strategy probably changed when the purchase was a new pair of shoes.

In addition, the strategy wouldn't necessarily work for your best friend with her parents, because every home and buying situation has a different dynamic. A mom or dad's ability to make or affect a decision varies from house to house and from decision to decision.

Selling in business isn't much different. Every company has a unique buying pattern. Decisions are made differently even in the same vertical market. People will be encountered during the buying process whose roles need to be identified. One of the common mistakes made by salespeople is to limit the evaluation of buying players to those within the organization. What is missed is the opportunity to leverage relationships from outside the corporate walls to help win the business.

You are probably now thinking this makes sense, but how do you break these down into meaningful categories or classes based on their roles in the buying process. In the next few sections, the buying players are separated into four distinct classes based on those roles. Those are "Beneficiary," "Wizard," "Saboteur," and "Mentor." This will create a new way to look at an organization. The overriding strategy for each new opportunity includes the quest to answer the following questions.

1. Who will benefit from your solution being adopted?

2. Who will ultimately award the contract?

3. Who is going to resist change?

4. Who is going to be the strongest ally in seeing that this solution is the one adopted?

The Beneficiary

One of the first people who will be encountered is the "Beneficiary." This group of buying players includes anyone and everyone who benefits from *your* solution being adopted. This is very different than saying it is composed of everyone who benefits from a *change* to his way of doing business. These buying players can fall within the prospect's organization, within the prospect's clients, or from outside the organization. The role of the salesperson is to identify all of the Beneficiaries because it is from this group that a "Mentor" is created. (More on Mentors later.)

For example, if the salesperson was facilitating the sale of a high-end copier that was faster, more reliable, and more cost-efficient than a prospect's current machine, there would be a number of Beneficiaries in the buying process such as:

♦ The Administrative Assistant, who has to stay at the copier because it keeps getting jammed during large copy jobs, would be a Beneficiary because her job would be made easier. She could work on other tasks as the copy job was produced.

- Since this solution would reduce the overall cost of copying, the Office Manager would be a Beneficiary because she is tasked with managing cost. Since the Administrative Assistant reports to her, she is also a Beneficiary because productivity can be improved.

- The CFO, who is always cost- and productivity-conscious would benefit for the same reason.

- Even the Vice President of Sales and Marketing would be a potential Beneficiary, as he was previously unable to deliver a proposal on time because the copier was broken.

Another way to add to the Beneficiary list is to research the company to find out their corporate goals and initiatives. If a provider's solution is not congruent with those, it will be a difficult battle to get the attention of the decision-maker, as they will have more important priorities than this one. This information can be ascertained in various ways. One is the corporate Web site. Another is through Hoovers or similar corporate research sites. However, the most effective way is to ask the buying players themselves. They are closest to the pulse of the organization and can provide the corporate flavor that is a critical piece in facilitating the buying process.

The Wizard

Simply stated, the "Wizard" is the buying player who will sign the contract. It is typically someone on the senior-management team with the ultimate buying power. In many instances, this person does not directly engage in the buying process. However, even though they may have another buying player facilitating the buying process, they are still the ultimate buyer.

The Wizard metaphor is a reference to the story of *The Wizard of Oz*. Recalling the movie, a large, booming voice echoed in the castle as this presence of power was depicted. However, a peek behind the curtain brought forth a benevolent individual. Dorothy wanted something, but so did the Wizard. The Wizard wanted to be understood. Once she understood what he wanted, she got what she wanted.

The salesperson's quest is to find out who is *hiding behind the curtain,* and determine the Wizard's agenda. Buying players have their own agendas although it is not always easy to ascertain them. One of my favorite expressions uttered by buying players is the "rubber-stamp decision." This is simply another sales mirage. How many times has a buying player said the following to you?

"This is definitely going to be awarded to you. I'm just waiting to get the official word from Mr. X. He just signs the contract."

Eventually, Mr. X gives his input and the deal unravels. Why? The Wizard was not engaged in the process. The most common reason for their lack of involvement is, much like Dorothy, salespeople are typically afraid of the Wizard. Don't believe it? Ask a fellow salesperson to describe Chief Financial Officers (CFOs), who are sometimes the Wizard in the buying process. Adjectives such as pleasant, friendly, and outgoing are rarely used to describe these folks. The adjectives heard are: tough, demanding, meticulous, and impersonal.

With this in mind, when the prospect says, "I'm going to go over this with the Big Boss and I'll let you know what he says," most salespeople do not pursue the conversation further. Because of the perception of the Wizard persona, they are reluctant to ask questions to understand and engage them in the buying process. This is a critical mistake and may result in the creation of a Saboteur in the buying process, as will be reviewed later. Quite frankly, failing to engage the Wizard is one of the sales pitfalls that results in a lost sale.

Key information to know about the Wizard:

1. What are the Wizard's main priorities and how does this solution fit within those?

2. How is the Wizard affected by the outcome of the decision?

3. What is important to the Wizard in making this decision?

4. What role will the Wizard play in making this decision?

5. If the Wizard were given a recommendation by the buying player team, what would prevent the Wizard from supporting it?

The Saboteur

Can you hear it? The eerie music playing in the background? Anxiety fills the air. The villain is about to enter. That's a certainty, but when? A few moments go by, yet no villain appears. It's coming and eventually, it does. All movies like this have a villain. All of a sudden, the villain jumps into the picture and scares the audience out of their seats! How did this happen? They knew there was a villain in the story and they even heard the villain's music!

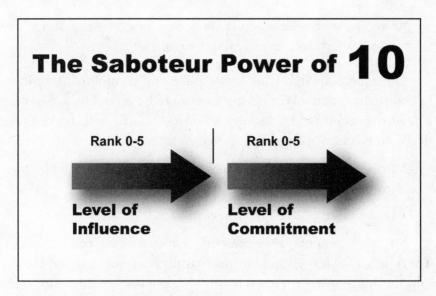

The Saboteur Power of 10

Rank 0-5

Rank 0-5

Level of Influence

Level of Commitment

Unfortunately, villains exist in every buying process. Not sometimes, *every* time! In stories, this villain exists for one reason: to make sure the protagonist (main character) does not get what they want. That is their sole job, their only reason for existence. This person is the "Saboteur" of the buying process. Think about your last few sales experiences. Do you hear the eerie music as you think about the Saboteur?

The Saboteur is the buying player, or dare I say *players,* who meet one, or many, of the following criteria:

- ◆ Favors the competition's solution
- ◆ Doubts your solution
- ◆ Favors status quo

Bottom line, this person is not on your team. The Saboteur is there to keep you from winning the business. In most scenarios, the

Saboteur can kill the deal, but cannot award it. However, Saboteurs attempt to negotiate, but from a weak position. They cannot offer the reciprocation of contact award if concessions are made. One clear way to flush this out is with the following question:

> "If we can make these adjustments, and I'm not suggesting that we can, will we be awarded the contract?"

The Saboteur will say he *cannot* make that commitment, unless of course, he is also a Wizard. In cases where he is not also a Wizard, a plan is needed before making a concession. To help make that decision, two introspective questions are asked:

♦ Does making this concession change the Saboteur to a Mentor (to be defined later)

♦ How does this affect later negotiations with the Wizard?

Not all Saboteurs are powerful. Some are just paper tigers. There is a two-step evaluation process used to quantify the influence of the Saboteurs. First is identifying the level of influence the Saboteur has in making the award. If the Saboteur cannot affect the buying decision or the other buying players in the process, the decision may be made to pay little mind to their concerns. To measure influence, a ranking of 0–5 is used, with five being the most influential, and zero being a completely non-influential buying player.

The second step is to determine the level of commitment to status quo or to another provider. Again, the 0–5 ranking is used, with five being the most committed to the alternative solution.

To be successful in dealing with the Saboteur, there are two options. The first option is to attempt to diffuse this person in the buying process so they cannot affect the decision. This is very difficult to do and can backfire. The most appropriate use of this option is if the Saboteur is from outside the organization or has little influence on the buying decision. For example, the Saboteur could be a longtime provider who will lose business as a result of a new contract award. In that scenario, diffusing them and their influence may be the only way to win. The "Mentor" can help to ensure that this outside influence does not create additional Saboteurs.

> ## Ignoring a buying player can turn them into a Saboteur.

That said, the first option is rarely used. Other than consultants, most organizations are more focused on their employees' perspectives than those of outsiders. Most of the time, a strategy is needed to work with the Saboteur. The key to dealing with them is to engage them in the process. Many Saboteurs are created by the sole fact that they feel left out of the process. Ego is one of the main creators of the Saboteur. The power to refuse to change when one does not get to vote is one of the ways the Saboteur rears it ugly head.

There are a variety of reasons why a person plays the role of the Saboteur. Sometimes, company politics create this entity. At other times, it can be a case of competing priorities. Worst of all, the salesperson is sometimes the one who creates a Saboteur because more love is shown to one buying player than another. Obviously, this is not a goal salespeople strive to achieve, but it's easy to fall into this trap. A friendly buying player is typically one on which a salesperson tends to focus, while he may actually be powerless in the buying process.

A hypothetical example: Two companies merge and seek to centralize their providers. The first group is buying office products from Office Products 'R' Us; the other group is buying from Super Office Products. The company has decided that one of these two companies will handle all office product needs. Both providers will be invited to address the combined group of buying players.

It's easy to see that there will be a winner and a loser in this process. Someone is going to have to change the way he is doing things. The key to winning the business will be to make sure everyone feels like he won. Ego will play a major factor in that no one wants to feel like he lost. The tougher the buying player, the more engaging him in the process becomes important. The way to do this is to take the time to understand his concerns and motivations. The goal is to help him to create the solution, so he moves from Saboteur to Mentor.

The Key to the Win!

With the pool of buying players identified, the next task is to identify those who are passionate about your solution and can influence the final decision. This is the *person on the inside* who will fight to the end for you. Why? If this solution is adopted, he wins. The ability to create a strong Mentor is the overwhelming factor in determining the winner of an opportunity. That's the magic! The entire award comes down to this element. There is one exception: The low-price provider can win without this relationship in place.

Effectively involving the Mentor in the buying process leads him to see the impact the solution can have on him personally. He takes ownership of the solution and convinces the other buying players that this is the best plan for the organization.

Wouldn't it be cool if Mentors were just found in the environment? Simply look around the room, make eye contact, and poof! There is a Mentor. Well, it doesn't quite work that way. Mentors are not found; they are created. They fall within the pool of buying players. While the Mentor is created, the salesperson wants to make sure he picks the right buying player. Who will make the strongest impact in the buying process? If he is selling an overall cost reduction, the CFO (also probably the Wizard in this case) makes an ideal candidate to consider.

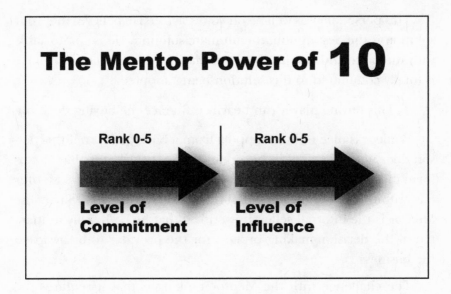

However, if the solution is designed to improve service, a key department manager may make the ideal Mentor. A mistake often made in identifying a Mentor is picking the friendliest buying player. He is the friendliest, responds favorably to the solution, but does not have the buying power to purchase a pair of socks.

Can there be too many Mentors? No. However, the focus is on identifying the *strongest* candidate, as this buying player will drive to the win. This quest starts at the beginning of the buying process and continues until the individual candidate is identified. In essence, each buying player is analyzed to see if he can, and will be, the strong Mentor. The evaluation process is very similar to that of the Saboteur. The difference is that the initial focus is on the level of commitment and then, the level of influence.

To qualify as a Mentor, a buying player must meet both of the following two criteria:

1. If the decision were entirely up to this person, he would award this the business to you...unequivocally.

This person may as well be on your payroll. He believes that your solution is the best option, the ultimate solution. He is comfortable with the price and can justify why it may be higher than others. He is totally committed to this solution being adopted.

2. This buying player can heavily influence the buying decision.

While it is nice to have support from a buying player, if this person does not have clout in his organization, he will not able to perform the role of the Mentor. The level of influence that the Mentor has within the organization is critical to the process. Since the Mentor is the internal seller, it is critical that he be heavily influential in the decision-making process for the provider to be awarded the business.

The challenge with the Mentor ranking is that it requires the salesperson to have introspective honesty. When in doubt, rank low. Finding a "10 Mentor" happens for one of two reasons: a rarity was found, or the salesperson was not truly honest with himself.

The mistake often made when analyzing commitment is not analyzing the impact of price. If someone cuts the provider's price by 20 percent, will the Mentor still be as committed as he was before? Will he buckle? Some Mentors are committed because they feel they are receiving the best price (not the best value) from the provider. But then a competitor arrives on the scene, offers a price reduction and the Mentor's loyalty sways (from you or to the competitor).

Scrutiny of influence is also daunting. Similar to the Saboteur, many Mentors position themselves as the "be all, end all" to the decision. In most corporate environments, this is rarely true. They will often say that their boss provides a rubber stamp on the deal. As discussed before, the rubber stamp is merely a sales mirage.

Whether the concern is influence or commitment, identifying the causes for concern is important. Does the Mentor have a neighbor who works for a competitor? Has a new buying player entered the scene? Is there a political battle? Salespeople are naturally optimistic.

I'm not a proponent of being a pessimist, but I *am* a supporter of the pragmatist philosophy. Since it will rarely, if ever, happen that a "10-Mentor" is encountered, rather than feel confident about the sale, ask the converse. What will prevent the sale from happening?

Since Mentors are not found, but are created, a process is needed to identify, create, strengthen, and coach. The Identification Test helps to identify a buying player with the potential to become the strong Mentor. With a candidate identified, the Creation Test is used to develop the candidate into a Mentor. The next test ensures that the Mentor is strong in their convictions with their internal buying team. Finally, coaching of the Mentor rounds out the process.

Identifying a Mentor Candidate

Finding the right Mentor candidate requires analyzing his level of influence in this buying decision. Since the goal is to select the best candidate, very specific questions will be asked of the candidate to understand his level of influence.

Mentor Identification Test

- If you were to find a solution that addressed your areas of concern, when would you (realistically) want to make a change?

- Why that date?

- What are the consequences if it doesn't happen by that date?

- What would a solution need to include for you to support making a change?

- What happens once you identify a solution that makes sense?

- When you make a recommendation to the organization, what usually happens?

Creating the Mentor

The questions above accomplish two main objectives.

◆ A candidate has been identified who is influential in the buying decision.

◆ An analysis has been performed to see how motivated this particular buying player is to making a change.

With a candidate identified, the next step is to transform him into a Mentor. Remember, Mentors are never found. Mentor *candidates* are found. A process facilitated by the salesperson creates Mentors. With this in mind, the following questions are asked to mold this buying player into a Mentor. All of the questions assume affirmative responses. Negative or vague responses are noted, as that affects his Mentor ranking. Oftentimes, an appropriate follow-up is "why?" This helps to understand his convictions.

Mentor Creation Test

◆ How does this solution compare to your current experience (and other competitors in the mix)?

◆ What are the key differences that you see in this solution?

◆ Are these differences significant enough for you to support a provider change?

◆ What could your current provider offer that would result in your staying with them?

◆ At this point, what is your recommendation to your organization?

◆ When you make a recommendation to the organization, what normally happens?

◆ What needs to happen for your recommendation to be adopted by the organization?

◆ Who will be involved from this point forward?

◆ What thoughts will they have regarding your recommendation?

◆ Why would they prevent you from going forward with this plan?

◆ If they do not support the change, what happens then?

Strengthening the Mentor

If all has gone well in the last step, a Mentor has been created. Congratulations! This buying player is influential in the buying decision, has clearly expressed his support for the prescribed solution, and can justify his decision. It is important that the Mentor be able to clearly describe the specific reasons for supporting the change, as the Mentor will be *selling* the plan to the other buying players. During this process, not only has "Mentor influence" been analyzed, but the barriers that could be imposed in the process have also been identified. Negative or elusive answers to any of the questions reduce the strength of the Mentor and exposes buying-process liability.

> ## A strong, well-coached Mentor
> ## is the key to winning!

The next challenge is strengthening the Mentor so that he is prepared to represent the solution to his colleagues. In some buying environments, this discussion is in a formal committee setting. In others, the process is more informal, and the Mentor is working individually with the other buying players to influence change. For the Mentor to be successful in getting what he desires, he requires coaching. In essence, he needs to learn how to sell.

Whether the committee is formal or informal, it is still a committee, meaning it is a multiple-person decision-making exercise. The challenge is that committees, in any form, are not trained on how to make decisions. Typically, decisions just stagnate and die while in committee. The decision-making process is usually vague. You may be envisioning a large boardroom with fifteen panelists, but this issue is true for a narrower scope as well. Remember, a committee can simply be one or two other buying players. However, the question of decision-making process remains.

To ensure obstacles are not encountered, the Mentor needs to be "strengthened" by helping him to see the potential speed bumps they may encounter. Without doing this, those speed bumps can become brick walls, also known as, "deal-killers"!

While to some, the "Mentor Strength Test" may seem invasive, the fact remains that without it, the deal will die. Some of you may be telling yourself that you could never ask these questions. It comes back to the earlier discussion of what motivates you. If you are truly trying to grab the prospect's wallet or just make commissions, it is no wonder that there is a feeling of discomfort. Certainly, the Mentor will feel that and the deal will die.

However, if your heart is focused on helping people reach their goals and desires, this exercise is much more understandable. You are helping them. Maybe the real question to ask yourself is, "What is my commitment to helping my clients achieve their goals?" With your heart focused on helping the Mentor, the following test is performed. By the end of the test, both the salesperson and the Mentor will see the potential speed bumps, be able to plan around them, and thus strategize to ensure the process continues as planned.

Mentor Strength Test

- How were the committee members selected for this evaluation?
- What role do you play on the selection committee?
- What are the main objectives of the committee?
- How does this solution tie in with the committee's main objectives?
- When was the committee formulated?
- What involvement did this group have in selecting the current provider?
- Who chairs the committee?
- Who are the members of the committee?
- For each person mentioned...

  What will he be looking for in a new solution?

  Why wouldn't he support the change?

  What happens if he doesn't support the change?

- How does the committee make decisions? (vote, consensus, loudest wins, and so on)
- What happens if they don't all buy into your recommendation?
- If the committee does not support your plan, what happens then?
- Assuming the committee supports your plan, what happens next?

Mentor Coaching

Sometimes all of the great work with Mentors can create a monster. The Mentor is so excited that he wants to run through walls to get the solution selected. Sometimes this energy causes fatal flaws in the buying process. Typically, the Mentor is not a professional sales-person and does not know how to sell their organization on their idea. The Mentor needs counsel on selling so they do not cause irreparable damage to the buying process.

The challenge with coaching the Mentor is doing so without offending this key support person. Challenge is the operative word here. Without careful planning to approach this discussion, it can easily result in offending the Mentor. Never a good thing.

To effectively coach the Mentor, the first step is again, an intro-spective exercise for the salesperson. What is the best path for the Mentor to follow *to get what he desires for his specific reasons?* Remember, if you accept that the role of the salesperson is to facil-itate the buying process resulting in your clients getting what they need and want, you can't help but to be successful. The two main areas that need sales coaching focus on managing the other buy-ing players in the process. These are engaging Beneficiaries and the Wizard.

When Beneficiaries are not engaged in the process, they may resent the Mentor's identified solution. This may occur for no reason other than that they felt left out of the process. In essence, the Mentor has created Saboteurs. The result: The Mentor loses. You and your Mentor lose.

Another example of this risk is when a corporate initiative is developed which impacts the field management in a company. There is an inherent strife between those two groups. Typically, corporate likes oversight and the field likes autonomy. Because of that, the field is ready to resist any and all corporate initiatives. Even the best-intentioned corporate Mentor will fail if they don't solicit input from their field constituency. This is needed even if the field-management team is not a member of the decision-mak-ing group. After all, they meet the criteria for Beneficiaries. They will resent being force-fed corporate programs even if these pro-grams benefit them. To avoid this peril, the Mentor engages the field management in crafting the solution, so they will feel like participants in the process and will buy-in when the solution is ultimately adopted.

Wizards can feel left out too. This is a problem, especially when the Wizard is the Mentor's boss. The Mentor, in trying to shine and gain stature within the organization, may not seek input from the Wizard on the solution. He will surprise the boss with his great plan. However, the Mentor will be the *recipient* of the surprise when the Wizard is resistant and skeptical to their idea. Why? The Wizard, because he was never offered the opportunity to provide input, will stall the process. This goes back to the rubber-stamp issue. There is no such thing as a rubber stamp. If you accept that rubber stamps are a sales mirage, you will never be surprised when the process does not go that way. Remember, the Wizard is a person, with thoughts, ideas, and, most importantly, accountability for this area of the business. He owns it, yet he has not been consulted on this initiative. The thought that his input was not solicited results in the very human reaction of resistance. At first, he will stall the decision. Once motivated to research the issue, he will begin looking at alternative solutions, and ultimately do one of two things. He will maintain status quo or pursue an alternative solution that he has developed. The Mentor loses; the sale is lost.

Coaching

While the goal may be clear, accomplishing the goal is not without potential pitfalls. Similar to the Beneficiary concern, it is very easy to offend the Mentor if this is not done with sensitivity. As a result, many salespeople wimp out and don't coach them. The eagle salespeople grasp the challenge and plan the approach to the conversation.

In the coaching process, *telling* the Mentor what to do is rarely effective. No one likes to be told what to do. Instead, the goal is to enlighten the Mentor so he can share how to best proceed. If performed correctly, the result will be an even stronger Mentor, as he will further recognize that the salesperson is trying to help him achieve his goals.

Consider a dialogue like this:

"Bill, I've been thinking about our approach and have some concerns. May I share them with you?" (Once accepted, continue.)

"I've been working with folks like yourself for a long time. At this point of the process, those folks elect to pursue one of two paths. If I can take a moment to describe these two..." (Once accepted, continue.)

"One path that is taken is for someone like yourself to engage all of the other key members of their team to gather their input to formulate the solution. This makes everyone feel like he has contributed and once the final solution is presented, they are all onboard. Thus, they get the solution they want. Quite frankly, these are the solutions that work best because everyone is onboard.

"The other path is the one where the "main person" works directly with me without any team involvement. We work hard to develop a plan that we feel everyone will support. Once the pièce de résistance is complete, the team is told about the solution that was developed. What typically happens is that he does not receive accolades for a job well done. Instead, he is greeted by resistance and skepticism for no reason other than the fact that these people felt left out of the process.

"This is what causes some concern. I may be wrong, but it feels like we may be going down the latter path. I feel obligated to share this with you, but am not sure of the best way to proceed and am looking to you for guidance. What should we do?"

Clearly, a message of support has been communicated to the Mentor. He will recognize that the salesperson has his best interests in mind. He will usually be receptive to coaching, and will begin to return to you for additional coaching. You have become the trusted advisor. The Mentor's commitment will elevate, as he will know you care about him, not his wallet.

Mentor Keys

The Mentor is one of the most overlooked parts of the buying process. Either the assumption is that the main contact is a true supporter, or that this main contact has a level of clout that does not exist. The reason the Mentor is a critical component to winning business is credibility within the organization. Salespeople are typically viewed as "peddling their wares," not looking out for the best solution for their customer, and selling whatever yields the biggest commission.

With that in mind, salespeople have a long road to hoe when it comes to building credibility with buying players. However, with a strong Mentor, an internal player who is looking out for the best solution for his company, there is an internal, trusted seller. Thus, the opinion of the Mentor is seen as more credible since he has nothing to gain by leading the company astray.

If one were to analyze sales "wins," one would typically find the following:

1. The most profitable sales and happiest clients had a strong Mentor in the buying process.

2. Sales "wins" which did not have a Mentor (or a weak one) were typically awarded based on low price.

In analyzing the losses, one of the following is typically true:

1. Each deal lost could be traced back to not having a strong, well-developed, and coached Mentor.

2. The Mentor did not have enough "political pull" to make the deal happen. This is evident when another salesperson wins the business because he worked with a higher-level person in the organization who became a stronger Mentor, i.e., senior- or executive-level management.

CHAPTER 9
With Roles Come Responsibilities

"People only see what they are prepared to see."
—Ralph Waldo Emerson

Putting This in Play

In the previous chapter, a new methodology was presented to profile the buying players in the account. Four distinct roles were identified (Beneficiary, Wizard, Saboteur, and Mentor) and introduced. The main concept behind those roles was for the salesperson to *size-up* every person met within the account to determine which role(s) that individual will play in the buying process. But who are these individuals who affect the buying decision for this specific offering? Who benefits from the solution? To best understand what makes these folks tick, a profiling exercise is conducted which will allow for identifying roles, understanding their challenges, and positioning the solution to a receptive audience.

> **A buying player usually plays
> multiple roles in the process.**

The exercise begins with the creation of a grid on a piece of paper with the title of everyone who is affected by the solution listed in the column headers. To do this effectively, the salesperson will want to expand his vision beyond those with whom he has worked histori-cally. The central question is: Who benefits or loses from this solution being adopted or not (Beneficiaries)? In essence, who are the poten-tial winners and losers? See the sample matrix below. List the titles of all of the buying players across the top of the matrix. I've included only four for this, but list all relevant ones. More is certainly better.

The left-hand column is for the profiling categories. These will be inserted as the chapter progresses.

Buying Player Matrix

	CFO	CIO	Procurement	Administration

Who Are These People?

With the buying players listed, the first step is to identify the role, or more commonly, *roles,* that each buying player may play in the selection process. The key is to identify all of the possible roles in the process.

For purposes of this exercise, the buying process for selecting a copier will be utilized. In this example, the administration staff may not possess the buying power of the Wizard, but could they be a Saboteur if the copier were too slow or unreliable? Could the Chief Financial Officer (CFO) serve as a Mentor if the solution reduced the dollars spent on copying? Absolutely! Could that same CFO also be a Saboteur if the copier costs 10 percent more than the current unit? Indeed! Could the Chief Information Officer (CIO) be a Mentor if the copier increased productivity for the company through its networking capabilities? Correct! While some can play multiple roles, rarely does someone play all four roles in a complex sale.

List all of the roles that each buying player may play within the process in the matrix.

Buying Player Matrix

	CFO	CIO	Procurement	Administration
Potential Role(s) in the Buying Process				

What Keeps Them Up at Night?

It would be egotistical to think that a provider's solution is the main thing on the minds of these folks. If this individual has been identified as being a participant in the process, it is safe to assume that the solution affects a piece of his world, but not necessarily his entire scope of responsibilities. If the solution is not a primary focal area for the Wizard or other influential buying player, the process has a high risk of failure. The question to ponder is: What keeps this buying player up at night? It takes a significant amount of research to fully understand his workplace challenges. Hopefully, the provider's solution is congruent with these challenges.

Revisiting the copier example, let's consider what keeps the CFO up at night. Here are just a few possibilities:

- The stock price if the company is publicly traded
- Shareholder value
- Profitability of the company
- Growing the company
- Managing cash flow
- Sarbanes-Oxley compliance
- Dealing with rising operational costs
- Provider consolidation

It is not often that a solution affects all of a buying player's workplace challenges. However, failing to match any of these challenges is cause for concern. If the benefits of the solution do not match any of these, the fundamental question becomes whether or not this individual is truly a buying player for this buying process. If so, more digging is needed to identify a potential match.

With that, how does selling a copier tie into those challenges? If the solution reduces the overall copying cost to the company, profitability ties in. If there is a creative way that the copier is financed, this could positively affect cash flow. It will be critical to the success of the process to align as many of the solution's benefits with what keeps these folks awake at night.

Insert all of the workplace challenges for the identified buying players in the matrix.

Buying Player Matrix

	CFO	CIO	Procurement	Administration
Potential Role(s) in the Buying Process				
Workplace Challenges				

What Do You Know, Joe?

Since the goal is to formulate a solution that is congruent with their focal areas, understanding the problems was the first step. Asking questions about those challenges becomes the next step. The question is: What do you want to learn from each of these buying players?

Returning to the copier scenario, the copier salesperson would probably want to learn the following from the CFO:

- How are they paying for the current copier and service?

- What are they paying now?

- Are there any perceived issues with the current provider?

- Where does the budget for copiers lie?

- What percent savings would the CFO need to see to support a change?

- Who are the other buying players who would be involved in this type of decision?

- What is their philosophy on working with providers?

Again, there are other questions which can be added to this list for the CFO. For each of the identified buying players, list what can be learned from them in the Education section of the matrix.

Buying Player Matrix

	CFO	CIO	Procurement	Administration
Potential Role(s) in the Buying Process				
Workplace Challenges				
Education				

What Language Do You Speak?

With a basic understanding of their challenges and the information that needs to be ascertained, an approach is needed to engage each buying player. The difficulty is that each one has its own nomenclature, its own language. Using the right language helps to build rapport with a buying player and shows an understanding of their business. Where many err is that they use the wrong language with the wrong players.

A great example of the language conundrum is in the health-club industry. A club member will ask if the club offers personal training. The trainer will say that they do, for $65 per hour. The member walks away frustrated. The club member was really asking for someone to set them up on a program, which is usually complimentary in clubs. In the personal trainer's vernacular, this question is tied to the club's hourly rate for providing ongoing support one-on-one to the members. Imagine this was how your buying player felt.

For the copier scenario, there is a high probability that the administration team is not primarily focused on the profitability of the company. Therefore, using financial language with them falls on deaf ears. The CFO, however, probably does not care that the red ink prints crisper than any other copier on the market today. These language disconnects can kill the sale. So, what is the CFO's language?

Some of the expressions that would relate to a CFO:

- P and L (profit and loss)
- Growth
- Budget
- Profitability
- Outsourcing
- Cosourcing
- Expense control
- Financial analysis
- ROI (return on investment)
- Net profit
- Cost containment
- Economy of scale
- Partner
- Sarbanes-Oxley (SOX)
- Internal Rate of Return (IRR)
- ISO/Six Sigma
- Supply chain
- Auditing

◆ Cost reduction ◆ Direct & indirect cost ◆ Measurement

◆ Staff reduction ◆ Accounts payable ◆ Metrics

For each of the identified buying players, list the terms associated with their role. One way to learn these is to review the Web sites associated with their trade journals and associations.

Buying Player Matrix

	CFO	CIO	Procurement	Administration
Potential Role(s) in the Buying Process				
Workplace Challenges				
Education				
Language				

Friend or Foe

Revisiting the subject of the Mentor, there were two criteria shared that the strong candidate must meet: heavily influential in the buying process and firmly committed to the provider's solution. This means that not every role qualifies as a Mentor, and some have a low probability of being that strong Mentor. While the administrative assistant may be excited about the solution, as it will make their job easier, she probably does not possess the level of influence to do anything about it. Every buying player has potential obstacles ranging from internal politics to lack of interest in this area of the business.

Continuing with the copier sale, the following obstacles may be associated with doing business with the CFO:

- Getting to him: Can he be reached to become engaged in the process?

- Balancing/competing priorities: Is this of interest to him?

- Time/interest: Does he have the time to focus on this project?

- Internal resistance: Will there be too much internal resistance to support the change?

- Not knowledgeable about copiers: Will he not engage because he doesn't know much about this part of his business?

- Push down/empowering subordinates: Will he not engage because he wants to leave this to others in the organization?

- Trust: Does he believe in the ROI for the solution that was presented?

In the matrix, list all of the potential obstacles that could prevent each buying player from becoming your strong Mentor.

Buying Player Matrix

	CFO	CIO	Procurement	Administration
Potential Role(s) in the Buying Process				
Workplace Challenges				
Education				
Language				
Potential Mentor Obstacles				

And What Are You Going to Do About It?

Identifying obstacles is always the first step in managing through them. One cannot fix problems that are not known. With a precise list of potential Mentor obstacles, the question becomes: What to do about them? Seeing the pothole in the road, how do you avoid driving into it? So, what's the plan to avoid the obstacles?

There were numerous reasons that would prevent the CFO from becoming a strong Mentor in the buying process. Some ways to address those are:

- ◆ Make only early or late calls to avoid gatekeepers, which improves the chance of reaching the CFO.

- ◆ Focus on global/visionary benefits of the solution using the CFO's language.

- ◆ Clearly tie the solution to the CFO's challenges.

- ◆ Align the solution with his strategy, vision, and corporate financials.

- ◆ Position ROI.

- ◆ Become a trusted advisor.

For each role, list the strategies to navigate around the obstacles. Sometimes, there won't be an effective strategy to resolve these. There's always one final option, which is to find other buying players to engage who have a higher probability of playing the role of the strong Mentor.

How Can You Help?

With a clear understanding of the buying player's world, the next step is much like child's play. It's the old game of matchmaking. What problems can be solved by your solution that ties to the workplace challenges of the buying player? This affects Mentor development, as the stronger the match, the greater the chance that this individual will be an advocate for the solution. The fewer the matches, the weaker the chance of this individual becoming a strong Mentor. There is also a high risk that this buying player could become a Saboteur, as they may prefer Status Quo.

Some of the synergies for the CFO participating in the buying process for the copier might be:

◆ Reduced cost through ROI

◆ Expense-control provisions

◆ Supplier reduction

◆ Internal staff reduction

◆ Productivity improvement

◆ Budgetary assistance

◆ Consolidated, centralized billing

While there are many other benefits that are afforded by the solution, each buying player is focused only on the ones that affect him. These may seem like buzzwords, but if used appropriately, they can strengthen the selection process.

Buying Player Matrix

	CFO	CIO	Procurement	Administration
Potential Role(s) in the Buying Process				
Workplace Challenges				
Education				
Language				
Potential Mentor Obstacles				
How Can You Help?				

For each of the buying players, identify all the synergies between the benefits of the solution and their workplace challenges.

Back to the Beginning

With all of this information compiled, the last step of the exercise is to revisit the sound-byte. All of this information allows for the formulation of a stronger sound-byte that can be customized for each buying player. It addresses their workplace challenges, in their language, tying to solution synergies.

The sound-byte elements for the CFO for a copier sale might be:

◆ On average, clients find a 16 percent reduction in their paper costs due to the efficiency-management system built into the software that is wonderful for expense control.

Buying Player Matrix

	CFO	CIO	Procurement	Administration
Potential Role(s) in the Buying Process				
Workplace Challenges				
Education				
Language				
Potential Mentor Obstacles				
How Can You Help?				
Sound-byte Elements				

- Cost per copy is reduced through the use of this patent-pending technology.

- Due to speed and reliability, clients also find they need fewer units, resulting in fewer dollars being spent on hardware purchases.

Insert the bullets that will be incorporated into your sound-byte for each of the identified buying players.

Putting It to Good Use

Gathering all of this information is daunting, a true pain in the neck. I get it. It comes back to just how good you want to be. I've seen many a salesperson keep this tool in their briefcase so they can refer to it before key meetings, when writing proposals, or even as a cheat sheet when cold-calling. It's a powerful tool! You have captured the information that will allow you to position yourself uniquely from the competition, another way to be different. One way to make the tool even better is to partner with colleagues and share the information. That way, you *all* win!

CHAPTER 10
Matchmaking

*"All truths are easy to understand once they are discovered;
the point is to discover them."*
—Galileo Galilei

Migrating From Vendor to Partner

Let's look at two restaurants: McDonald's and Morton's of Chicago. When someone goes to McDonald's, they go because they are hungry. When someone goes to Morton's of Chicago, they want a dining experience. McDonald's offers value meals. Morton's is probably not for those concerned about price. The McDonald's experience involves ordering a meal and the order is provided quickly and accurately. The question asked of every order at McDonalds is, "Would you like fries with that?" (Apparently, fries go with everything.) At Morton's, the wait staff make initial recommendations to the diner, listen to the order, make additional recommendations based on the initial dining selections, finish receiving the order, and return with a stellar meal. While both are successful restaurant chains, this is a great metaphor for the vendor/partner relationship experienced in sales.

In the movie *Wedding Crashers,* true love is defined as the soul's recognition of its counterpoint in another. Wouldn't it be great if partner relationships worked the same way? Well, they can and do. When true business partnerships are formulated, both parties grow as a result. But how is a match found?

As a salesperson, it is all about the mindset. If the goal of the salesperson is selling something to someone, the likelihood that he will formulate partnerships is nil. His mindset is about peddling his wares, not understanding and solving business problems. Business partnerships come together by identifying the synergies between organizations resulting in strong benefits for both. Thus, the eagle salesperson serves the role of the matchmaker.

> **Vendors have customers,
> while partners have clients.**

The mindset of a matchmaker is very different than that of the traditional salesperson. Matchmakers wake up each morning with the goal of finding common bonds with business associates. Take Velcro, for example. The tighter the bond between the two surfaces, the more difficult it is to separate them. Thus, the ideal business partnership is created.

But what does it take to do this well? First, the salesperson has to master his half of the equation. He needs to know every bit of what his company does and who the right audience is for it. He also needs to understand industry challenges and issues impacting his clientele. To this day, I continue to be shocked at how few salespeople throw themselves into their business. They don't make the investment to master their craft. They don't join and get active in their industry associations. They don't fully understand their solution from a global perspective. The eagle salespeople are often confused for industry experts because they understand the pertinent issues impacting their clientele. They have invested time to study and learn what is important to their clients, and have mastered those elements. Most salespeople never do this. They continue to repeat the same boring sales mantra over and over again: "Can I have your business, please?"

The second element is the ability to ask key questions of the potential business partner and synthesize the shared information. Launching questions into the air and failing to process the information is a commonly made mistake. When preparing for the meeting, it is helpful to know the questions to be asked and the possible responses that might be heard. Preparation can then be done to direct the conversation appropriately based on those responses. Many salespeople ask questions with little or no purpose. Can you imagine a litigation attorney doing that? Never! They only ask pertinent questions to which they usually know the answer. If they ever ask a question that is not relevant, the opposing attorney objects and the objection is sustained by the judge. Sales doesn't have a judge, or an opposing attorney. Asking pointless questions can ruin rapport, and thus, the sale. There are just so many questions that someone will tolerate, so asking the most relevant ones is vital. Again, proper preparation on the part of the salesperson will help to avoid this peril.

Game Preparation

When I graduated from high school, I was still a little guy. I was 5'10" and about 110 pounds. I decided to join a gym, a habit that has stuck with me for over twenty years. I started out clueless, as most do. I didn't know how to use the equipment. Nor did I know what body parts to exercise together. Form? To me, form was a piece of paper, not a method of performing an exercise correctly. And I thought that only the nerds in the gym carried a notebook and wrote down what they were doing.

After a while of not getting results, I met a personal trainer who had successfully competed in bodybuilding. His first question for me was what my plan was when I arrived at the gym. Looking at the girls in the aerobics class was not the answer he was looking for. The truth was that I had no plan. I showed up, looked around the gym, and chose random pieces of equipment to use. He told me that that my planning matched my results. No plan, no results. I couldn't argue with him.

He then asked me if I felt I was improving in the gym. Was I getting stronger? How many repetitions did I perform the last time I did pull-ups? I had no clue. "How can you progress if you are not measuring your performance?" he asked. "How do you know if you are being successful? How will you know it's time to push yourself to the next level?"

After this discussion, I went out and bought a notebook in which I began to document every workout. From the exercises I performed in the order that I performed them, to the number of repetitions I performed in each set, I noted it all. Each time I worked out, I looked back at past workouts and either added resistance to the exercise or strived to add one repetition more than the last time. A few months later, I saw that trainer again. He didn't ask if I was making progress. He *told* me I was making progress. He could see the difference. He saw my confidence in the gym, as well. When I got to the gym, I already had a plan. In the course of the last twenty years, I've competed in bodybuilding and power lifting (all natural) and still write down every workout, set, and repetition. If I needed a spot (assistance), I documented that as well.

I see this same mistake often made by salespeople—not rookies, veterans. It seems like such a basic thing to do, but it is just not done. They show up at a meeting with a prospect, have the meeting, and leave. Was it a good meeting? How would they know? There was no plan. This leads to the discussion of formulating an effective needs analysis program. That program is based on one fundamental principle:

> "What information is needed from the prospect and when is it needed?"

> **Identifying the specific problem(s) that the buying players want resolved is the key to formulating a powerful solution.**

If it's qualifying the prospect, what information is needed to qualify? If it's opportunity scoping, how is that quantified. All along the way, the salesperson is challenging himself to measure the success of the program. If it worked, to what was that attributed? If not, why didn't it work and what will be done differently next time? That introspection leads to personal growth. If the plan worked, what can be replicated in another buying process? The true litmus test question is:

"The plan was a success if *what* happened?"

With this in mind, the remainder of this chapter will walk you through the development of your own needs analysis program. Just like the other concepts shared in this book, it fails if you don't hold yourself accountable for measuring success along the way.

Dialogue Facilitation

The term "needs analysis" is probably not new to you. You've undoubtedly heard it hundreds of times from various managers, books, articles, and journals. I'm assuming most, if not all of you, agree with the concept wholeheartedly. Me, too! The struggle is actually putting one together. Having never done it, it can be a daunting task. With a dodo sales manager, don't expect one to be handed to you either. It's left to you to figure it out. Relax. In this chapter, you will learn how to formulate a powerful needs analysis program even though you've probably never done it before.

One use of a needs analysis program is to understand a prospect's situation in a way that allows for the formulation of a winning solution. It is important to note that a presented solution without a problem identified by the buying player is meaningless. So a needs analysis that yields no problems is either poorly executed or identifies a lack of opportunity. More often than not, it is a poor needs analysis that is the issue here.

Many salespeople confuse lecture for needs analysis. "I told them that we offered the state of the art in gadget-making and she smiled." This is an example of a confused salesperson who thinks that lecturing is positioning. Most people want to be led on a path to a solution, as opposed to being told the best thing to do. That's why I call it a "buying process" instead of a "sales process." This cannot be accomplished through lecture. It is done through the facilitation of the dialogue of interest. Unfortunately, sometimes this is forgotten, and the salesperson creates a soliloquy.

At the other end of the spectrum is the interrogation approach where the only thing missing at the meeting is the spotlight on the prospect. "Where were you on the night of...?" is not a very comfortable experience. This is caused by a salesperson rapid-firing questions at the buying player. Many don't even listen to the responses. They are just waiting for the opportunity to ask the next question. Asking questions in a buying process is an art form. Thus, I refer to this as the "art of query." It is a skill that many have not mastered. The art of query requires salespeople to use various question types based on the situation. To be effective at it, planning, strong listening skills, and the ability to quickly identify the appropriate question for the situation is needed. Asking or not asking key questions at the right time can make or break the opportunity too. For example, asking a prospect whom else they are considering for their business could cause them to look at other providers when they had not planned to do so. At other times, not asking that question jeopardizes the sale.

Insulators help create rapport.

Effective facilitation includes asking strategic questions and processing the response. As if figuring out the appropriate questions was not challenging enough, these questions need to be posed in the buyer's dialect, which was shared in an earlier chapter. This means that questions are asked using words, phrases, and expressions consistent with the buying player's specific job and industry language. Failure to match language can result in a major disconnect between the salesperson and the prospect, similar to speaking Chinese to a Frenchman.

Insulators

The key to effectively opening and maintaining this dialogue is the use of "insulators." These are expressions that soften questions and create a comfortable, conversational environment that encourages open conversation. They are used as buffers both before and/or after asking questions. Once the insulator is in place, the question is asked in a casual, non-threatening way to begin an interactive dialogue. One of the concerns that salespeople often have is that the buying player could perceive a question as invasive or feel uncomfortable responding openly to it. This is certainly a valid concern. Asking questions at the wrong time or without the appropriate insulator can destroy all rapport. The insulator serves as the question-buffer so that the buying player feels more comfortable responding.

Language is a tricky tool, too. This is best shown with the use of "but" (spoken or inferred) as a part of an insulator. It can dramatically affect the message. This expression negates everything spoken prior to it.

"You are the most beautiful person in the world, but your hair is always messy."

The only thing heard by the person at the other end of this conversation is that the speaker has a problem with her hair. Amazingly, the speaker has paid a huge compliment that has gone unheard. However, "but" can begin the insulator after a question and be rather effective. This means it would be very effective after a question, but not before one.

Some examples of insulators before a question are:

◆ I'm not quite sure how to phrase this…

◆ Forgive me if this sounds direct. May I ask you about…

◆ I don't know if this would make sense for you. What about…

◆ I don't suppose you want to discuss…

◆ Just out of curiosity…

◆ Just a thought…

Some examples of insulators following a question are:

◆ …the reason I asked was…

◆ …which is why I was asking.

◆ …not to put you on the spot.

◆ …but this may not make sense for you.

To share a personal aside, I am originally from the East Coast where communication is very straightforward. If an idea can be conveyed in a few words, it is. Living in the Midwest, I've found the communication requirement to be very different. Especially in e-mail, I can't overstate the importance of using insulators as part of the written medium. Without it, it is very easy to convey a message other than what was intended. As someone who has personally been burned by this, I share this nugget.

The Art of Query

With the insulators in place, the next step is to formulate questions, but what questions? In what order? What information is needed? Each question type is appropriate during certain phases of the buying process. Not sure where to start with formulating a list of questions? Pull out the buying player grid and review the "education" row. These are the aspects that you have already determined that you need to know from each specific buying player. It can provide a core for the needs analysis for a particular buying player.

"Rapport questions" are used to create a comfortable setting for the buying player. Many salespeople skip this type of questioning or fail to use them in a genuine way. This leads to trust issues throughout the process. They are used at the early part of the interaction with a buying player. They include, but are not limited to, questions about the prospect's tenure, responsibilities, department, and organization goals. These questions serve as a transition between walking into someone's office and getting into a hardcore business discussion, as well as providing some dialogue direction.

Some examples are:

- How long have you been with the organization?
- What are your primary responsibilities?
- What are the goals of your department for this year?

"Data collection questions" help to identify the key pieces of data needed to understand the opportunity. The responses to these questions will provide critical pieces of data that will be used to formulate other types of questions. These are questions that ask how many, how much, who is your current provider, and so on. These questions are often used to qualify an opportunity.

A tactical gaffe is asking imposing data collection questions too early in the process. The indicator of this is that the prospect declines to answer. If the right has not been earned to ask certain questions through rapport building, the entire process can crumble. Proper call planning will help to identify what is considered an invasive data collection question to be saved for a more opportune moment. The two data collection questions considered most invasive involve current pricing and provider satisfaction levels.

As a first step in formulating your specific needs analysis program, identify all of the data that is needed to be known and when it is needed to be known. What data is needed to:

- Qualify the opportunity
- Formulate a solution
- Develop pricing
- Understand the buying process
- Understand the competitive landscape
- Determine the appropriate positioning questions

"Challenge questions" expose areas that the buying player feels could be improved. These may be due to a current provider's shortcoming or something that has never been addressed before. Challenge questions are an effective tool to use during an initial consultation to determine if there is a potential match between the provider's capabilities and the buying player's needs/requirements.

Some examples are:

- If there were one area of your program that could be better, what would it be?
- What are some of the challenges you have had with your program?
- If you could create the ideal solution, what would it include?
- What three areas could be improved?
- If you could wave a magic wand, what three things would you want to see improved in your service program?

With a challenge(s) identified, the next step is to analyze the buying player's interest in resolving the challenge(s). In essence, an understanding is needed of the answers to the following questions:

- What has been done to address that challenge and by whom?

- What were the results of that effort?

- Who is impacted by the challenge and why?

- What is the level of importance in resolving this issue.

- When does he want it resolved?

By the conclusion of the analysis of interest, what will be known is:

- The buying player's main challenges

- The priority of these challenges

- What he has done about them

- Who the challenges impact

- What has been done to solve the challenges

- When he would like to see the challenges addressed

- How he would solve the challenges

Positioning Differentiation

With a clear understanding of the perceived challenges, the next step is to incorporate positioning questions into the conversation. This is the most difficult tool for salespeople to use. It requires the ability to refrain from soapbox lectures and to lead the prospect to express an interest in a strength of his through query. It is a unique method for differentiation. From the information learned from rapport, data collection, and challenge questions, areas are identified that could be improved for the prospect by the provider's solution. The buying player has not specifically identified these as areas of potential improvement or vocalized a desire to address them. Perhaps, he did not know it could be improved, or he is satisfied with the status quo.

> **Positioning questions expose areas of potential improvement that the buying player did not already perceive and are advantages of your offering.**

While it appears that challenge and positioning questions are very similar, there is one fundamental difference. Challenge questions expose areas that a buyer has identified for potential improvement. Positioning questions expose areas of potential improvement that the buying player did *not already perceive* and *are advantages of your offering*.

Consider someone who goes to the dentist because they have pain in their molars. While the dentist is handling the cavity in the molar, he discovers issues in other teeth that require a root canal. The patient knew about the molar issue, but was unaware of the other issues. The dentist has identified an area that needs to be addressed, but the patient was not aware of the problem. That's what positioning questions do for a salesperson. They expose areas of improvement that the buying player had not necessarily perceived as being sub par.

Positioning allows the prospect to openly share information. At the same time, it prevents the salesperson from focusing too closely on one aspect of their offering, when the prospect hasn't yet indicated that he shares this concern. There are three common mistakes made during positioning:

1. Asking close-ended (yes/no) questions

2. "Lecturing" before the prospect indicates he is interested in discussing that attribute

3. Failing to use insulators

Making these errors—in essence, pushing what is thought of as important before hearing what the buying player values—will leave the buying player feeling that he was not understood, or that there was no interest in trying to understand his unique situation. More importantly, he will be justified feeling this way. Translation: lost opportunity.

To effectively use positioning, there is a five-step process to undergo:

Step 1: Identify unique advantages of your company, your offering, and you.

Step 2: Define the problems solved by these advantages.

Step 3: List the discussion points leading to the opportunity to ask the positioning question.

Step 4: Formulate the positioning question.

Step 5: List the key aspects of the advantage to discuss upon receiving a positive response.

The result of this exercise is another important tool that is helpful to keep on hand at all times. It is your specific differentiation guide. It will help when making prospecting calls. It will help as a pre-game review before a key meeting. Quite frankly, I'm not sure when it is *not* needed.

Using positioning questions leads the buying player to the conclusion that this product is unique, and that its very uniqueness is something they must have. Consider a furniture sale. The furniture is available in a plethora of colors. This attribute is unique to this furniture and provides a competitive advantage in the marketplace. The problem that this solves is that it provides options, which is especially important when trying to furnish a room where the color pattern has already been developed.

With a clear picture of the advantage and the problem it solves, what are the discussion points that lead up to this question. In this scenario, the salesperson might discuss the color of the buying player's carpeting, favorite colors in the home, and whether they have small children or pets.

All of these points lead the conversation down the path to prepare for the positioning question. Using the positioning model, a line of query like this would be used beginning with an Insulator:

Insulator: "Many of our clients find their options limited when trying to buy furniture for rooms that already have the color-pattern developed. We often hear that from our clientele."

What's unique? Unlike anyone else in the market, our furniture can be produced in a wide array of colors.

What problem is solved? It provides our clients with options, especially important when trying to furnish a room where the color pattern has already been developed.

Discussion points: Color schema, kids, pets, etc.

Positioning question: "What experiences have you had in trying to match the existing color-pattern in the rooms with the new furniture you are considering?"

Key aspects: color flexibility, etc.

The final step is completed once the prospect has expressed difficulty with this issue and is interested in hearing solutions. At that point, the details of the differentiated solution are discussed.

The final part of positioning is the "analysis of interest." Once the buying player has responded favorably to the positioning question, the next step is to determine his interest in addressing this new issue. It cannot be assumed that someone wants to solve every problem, nor can it be assumed which problems he wants solved.

With a positioning point(s) identified, the next step is to *analyze the buying player's interest* in resolving it/them. In essence, an understanding is needed of the answers to the following questions:

◆ What has been done to address this and by whom?

◆ What were the results of that effort?

◆ Who is impacted by this and why?

◆ What is the level of importance in resolving this issue?

◆ When does he want it resolved?

Wrapping Up the Meeting

Anytime I meet with a buying player, I have different goals. The one that is consistent in every one of my meetings is the goal of creating an environment whereby buying players feel comfortable being completely honest with me. Everything else is secondary and varies based on the type of meeting.

When I am packing up my briefcase, I like to ask one last question with an insulator:

"I'm sure you've talked to others who provide similar solutions; what did we share today that was different than what you have seen or heard?"

This gives great insight into the value he saw (if any) in this meeting. It will also help to provide future direction for the process.

CHAPTER 11
Ah...The Best Laid Plans...

"You will never do anything in this world without courage. It is the greatest quality of the mind next to honor."

—Aristotle

Expecting the Unexpected

I wish I could say that if everything was done exactly as presented that you would win 100 percent of the accounts you pursued. Well, oftentimes, this not quite the case. Things will go awry. A word of advice: Don't look for reasons why you will win, look for areas of vulnerability. Something was missed along the way. Perhaps all of the necessary buying players were not engaged. Maybe there was a question that should have been asked and wasn't. The circumstances with the buying team may have changed.

Here's the thing: Looking for reasons to be optimistic creates sales blind spots. The risk of being the recipient of a less-than-pleasant surprise increases significantly. Looking for risks removes the blind spots, allowing for the creation of strategies to address the vulnerabilities. Again, I'm not suggesting that salespeople change from optimists to pessimists. It's the pragmatist view that removes the blind spots, in essence, the logical thinking without emotion clouding vision.

The best way to implement the pragmatist way of thinking is to prepare for the unexpected. Or, dare I say, prepare for the expected.

In today's high-tech world, it is commonly known during prospecting, that there is a better-than-50-percent chance of ending up in voicemail. Yet, few salespeople develop powerful voicemail messages from their sound-byte. Certain concerns will arise in the buying process. Price will almost always be a discussion point, yet, few prepare adequately for it. Deals will get stuck for a variety of reasons. The salesperson will know what needs to be done, but their Mentor wants to proceed differently. How does the salesperson change course without offending their Mentor?

> **Salespeople who adopt a pragmatist philosophy will win more business as they will expect the unexpected.**

Perhaps today a phone call will be received from a buying player saying you made the short list of providers being considered. Great news, I think. But what information is needed to prepare and deliver the winning presentation? Perhaps the finish line is in sight and the Mentor asks for references. What is the best way to satisfy this request? What strategy is needed for this key component of the buying process? Or maybe they want to try before they buy.

This chapter will help with preparation for the expected, and the dreaded unexpected.

Getting Unstuck

The salesperson knows exactly what they want their Mentor to do, but he won't do it. Sound familiar? Stuck, like a fly on flypaper. The knee-jerk reaction is to tell the Mentor what to do and drag them to the finish line. This works sometimes, but not often. It's also painful for both the salesperson and the buying player. The dilemma is how to get buying players to do what the salesperson desires for the buying player's reasons, so the salesperson gets what he desires for his. The key is to invert the previous sentence. A better read is, "If my Mentor gets what he desires, I will get what I desire." This philosophical change is the means of motivating prospects to take action. No one wants to be pushed. He wants to be motivated. For those of you who are parents, it comes as no surprise that "pushing" doesn't work any better with children than adults.

Where many salespeople have challenges is not knowing why their buying player should be inclined to do what they want them to do. One of the most common examples of this is when a salesperson wants to be introduced to other buying players in the organization. I've been asked by countless salespeople how to effectively do it. The secret lies in a question: Why introduce you to others in the organization and how does this help the buying player? The answer to that two-part question is the secret of how to do it. If the Mentor is creating the solution without the involvement of others who will be affected by it, they run a high risk of being rejected. By collaborating on it with their peers, the probability of acceptance grows immensely. Knowing that, the salesperson plans a discussion to help the Mentor see this risk. Oftentimes, salespeople don't use this thought process. They ask for an introduction and are rebuffed. Worse, they tick-off their Mentor because they are offended by the request to meet others. "This decision is mine."

Since the role of the salesperson is to facilitate the buying process, he has an obligation to address areas of concern with the process. If he spots an iceberg in the water, he best inform the captain and quick! With this thought process in mind, the exercise below lists some of the areas whereby a salesperson has reached a crossroad. The first column of the table below describes what is desired of the buying player. The second column is for the reason why the buying player should do what the salesperson suggests. With those two pieces of information identified, a strategy can be developed to motivate the buying player to do what is best at this phase of the process. As I shared before, the overall goal with buying players is to create an environment whereby they feel comfortable being totally honest. However, many salespeople fear this honesty, as they will hear things they don't want to hear. "If I can wait six months to hear that we are not going to get the business, that's the plan for me. I can still keep it on my forecast."

Reframing Workshop

What you want the buying player to do.	Why should they do it?	What will you say to motivate your buying player to take the requested action?
Return a phone call.		
Agree to a meeting with you.		
Take an interest in your story despite being happy with his current provider.		
Introduce you to other buying players.		
Bring other buying players into the process.		
Become forthcoming with requested information.		
See the difference between you and the competition.		
Stick to the agreed-upon timeline and action items.		
Not be inclined towards status quo.		
Make a decision.		

Unfortunately, business leaders don't share that philosophy. Being straightforward with a buying player can help to best understand roadblocks and challenges within the organization. Take, for example, a scenario whereby a buying process has become protracted. For months, the process is stuck at the final hurdle, a decision. Days have become weeks, weeks have become months, and still no decision. Stuck! One way to motivate the buying player is sharing what I call the "heart and head" strife. It is an open and honest request for guidance.

"I am wondering if I can share something with you." (With acceptance, proceed.)

"I've been thinking about our relationship and I'm torn. You and I have worked very hard to craft the solution for the organization. My heart is telling me that this will eventually be the solution adopted. My head is telling me that if this were going to come together, it would have happened by now. You have been so open with me about why you want this to happen and I appreciate that. So, I'm at a point where I don't know the best thing to do to help you, and I'm looking for your guidance. What do you suggest?"

This communicates the caring the salesperson has in trying to help their Mentor get the solution he wants adopted. This opens the door for an open and honest dialogue, and hopefully, the development of a strategy to create action. But what happens when the buying player wants to proceed one way and the salesperson wants to proceed another way.

Disconnects

Disconnects in any relationship can lead to its unraveling. They are very difficult to manage, though if not managed, the deal can be lost. What a conundrum for a salesperson! The salesperson wants the buying player to do one thing; the buying player wants to do another. Ugh! What to do when how he wants to proceed differs from what the salesperson feels is best?

The key to doing this is using a tool I call "reframing." This is where the buying player cedes to the salesperson and changes his point of view. The goals become aligned. A great example of this occurs during prospecting calls. The salesperson requests a meeting. The buying player requests a price over the phone instead. If the salesperson refuses, they lose. If he agrees to provide the price over the phone, the buying player will make his decision with less than all of the relevant information, which means a probable lost sale. The salesperson needs to help the buying player to see the benefits of the meeting so that the buying player suggests that this is a much better way to proceed. Unfortunately, I cannot provide the answer to the benefits of that meeting. Hopefully, you can. The following is an example of how to formulate a response to a premature pricing request.

> "As you can probably imagine, I get asked that question all of the time, and I appreciate your asking. Did you know that there are over 200 different programs with varying price points? At this time, I don't know enough about you or your needs to recommend one of them so I will give you the highest price. Or, if I could make a suggestion (insulator), I could come out and visit with you to best understand your needs. From that discussion, I could provide the best price for the right program for you. How would you like to proceed?"

In that dialogue, the unpalatable suggestion of providing the highest price is suggested. Who wants the highest price? By accepting meeting, the salesperson can provide the best price for the right program. The buying player probably doesn't know all of the options and choices in determining the right program. The salesperson does. In his heart, the salesperson knows that he cannot help his buying player if he doesn't first understand their needs, wants, and desires.

In the exercise below, eight common requests from buying players are listed in the first column. The second column lists what the salesperson desires instead. The last column is the reframe of why this is the best next step.

Disconnects Workshop

What they want	What you want	Resolution
A price over the phone.	A meeting.	
A proposal without dialogue.	A conference call to review the proposal.	
A price now.	To frame your approach before pricing.	
Match the lowest price I have on my other proposals.	Award at proposed rate.	
Meet with me again.	Involve the other buying players.	
Pricing by component.	Pricing by composite.	
Present to my committee members.	A worthwhile, productive meeting which leads to a contract award.	
Unknown	Award the contract that appears to meet all of their needs.	

The Finalist

"Great news! You've been selected to present to our committee on your solution for our company." Music to the salesperson's ears! Unfortunately, many salespeople forget everything that they have been taught about facilitating the buying process when they hear the news. The response is typically, "Great, when can we come?" However, to effectively formulate and present a solution, the salesperson needs to fully understand this step of the process.

In addition, there are two schools of thought about when to present, and both have merit. Some say that it's best to go first to raise the bar higher than the competition can reach. Make the first impression! Others argue that the best time slot is the last one. This allows the team to address anything that may have been presented by the competition. Make the final impression! A case can be made for either. Most agree that it's best not to have a presentation slot that is in between the competitors, and always avoid the late afternoon slot on a Friday. If the first time slot is given, one of the best ways to ensure that no one trumps the offering is to schedule a debrief call with the Mentor for after all of the presentations have been completed. This is scheduled during the notification of the assigned presentation time slot as opposed to trying to schedule this time post-presentation This allows the salesperson to address any vulnerabilities that may have been created by the competition.

With the presentation time set, how does one best prepare? What is the best solution to present? What team is needed for the presentation? With all great questions, the answers lie within the prospect. This is a time when a strong Mentor is essential. The Mentor will provide great insight because he wants this solution to be the one adopted by the organization. Procurement officers rarely share the needed critical information. Without the strong

Mentor in place, it is nearly impossible to adequately prepare. The first step to preparation is an introspective analysis of the buying situation.

- How many Mentors have been created?

- Who is the strongest Mentor?

- What is his level of commitment to you?

- How influential is he in the buying decision?

- Who are the Saboteurs?

- What is their level of influence?

- How committed are the Saboteurs to their beliefs?

- What has been learned during the needs analysis program?

- What aspects of the solution are most important and to whom?

Having identified the strongest Mentor, your next step is to profile the committee. Remember, committees are not formulated to make decisions. They are usually a bunch of people assigned to a project. What's scary for the salesperson is that they rarely have a defined process to evaluate providers and make a decision. This was covered in detail in the Mentor section of the book. To best understand the committee, the following information is requested of the Mentor.

- What role do you play within the committee?

- What is your recommendation to the committee?

- Why is *that* your recommendation?

- What was it about the written response (RFP) that led the committee to select you as a finalist?

- Why are those things important to them?

- Whom do those issues impact?

- What did they see in others' responses that was not well-addressed to you?

- Why are those things important to them?

- Whom do those issues impact?

- What involvement did this group have in selecting the current provider?

- What are the topics that they want addressed during the presentation?

- Why are those important and to whom?

- How much time will be given to present the solution?

- How many people will be at the presentation?

- Is there anyone who is heavily influential in the provider-selection process who won't be at the presentation?

- What departments will be represented?

- What will they be looking for in a new solution?

- Who chairs the committee?

Most times, the finalist process includes multiple groups presenting to the committee. However, there is always the possibility of no decision being made, which means that status quo wins. Most companies will not openly disclose the list of competitors. However, a strategic inquiry facilitated by the salesperson can yield key information to help prepare.

- How many groups are being invited to present?

- Has the company made the firm decision to change providers?

- What is driving that decision?

- What is most important to the committee in selecting a new provider?

- What concerns do they have that they want to make sure are addressed, i.e., implementation, etc.?

- Was there anything that the competition addressed in their solution that was not addressed in yours?

- Do you have the first/last time slot?

Understanding the committee dynamic...

- How does the committee make decisions, i.e., vote, consensus, loudest wins, etc.?

- On what criteria will the providers by judged?

- How will the criteria be measured?

- What is the priority of those?

- Why were those selected as the criteria?

- What role does price play in the final decision?

- What is the next step after the presentations?

Some housekeeping tips to help prepare:

- Make sure that the entire team has clear driving directions to the site.

- Arrive at least 30 minutes early to allow for any setup needs.

- If a projector is being used, confirm that the client has one and that it is compatible with the laptop being utilized.

- If the Internet is needed, confirm that firewalls do not prevent access for noncompany-owned computers.

- Determine roles for the presentation to avoid a free-for-all environment. One member of the team serves as the facilitator and the others support that role.

Trials and Pilots

It looks like things are progressing. A call is received from the Mentor that sounds like this:

"This sounds great! Here's what we want to do. We want to try your service for free for thirty days. If that goes well, we will talk about plans to go forward."

Call the sales manager! This one is done. It's a victory! Ring the bell! These are all common responses from salespeople to what is perceived as account progress. However, dissecting the request shows that the sale is not as "done" as it may look.

First, they want to "try" the service. "Try" infers that they may not believe the presented benefits. It may also mean that they are coming out of a bad experience with another provider and don't want to make the same mistake twice. There is a definitive trust issue here, which needs resolution. Without understanding the cause for concern, it will be difficult, if not impossible, to diffuse.

What do you do if a trial does not allow for demonstration of differentiation? For example, if your forte is account management, how will a short-term trial allow for demonstration of that? Working in that type of business, the salesperson can't let a pilot happen. Saying "no" gets them knocked out of consideration. Saying "yes" won't help them win either. It's another example of the need for "reframing." What can be shared with the buying player that helps them to feel good about not getting what they want? Sounds like an exercise from earlier in the book. The key is to understand what the prospect wants to accomplish from the pilot. If the company cannot accomplish its goals, the point becomes moot.

"Free." We all would like something for free. We don't often get it. What value does free really portray to a prospect? Zero!

Something to think about, if they want to analyze billing as a part of the evaluation, how will "free" accommodate for this element. If they are trying to reduce risk, there are a number of ways to mitigate that. For example, a money-back guarantee can be offered based on the success metrics of the program. Keep in mind that pilots and trials always have a cost to your company.

One of the push backs that buying players will offer is that the competition is willing to do this for free. Every time I hear that, I'm reminded of my mother asking me, "If Brian jumped off the Brooklyn Bridge, would you?" Maybe the buying player needs to be advised that the free pilot will be worth everything he paid for it. If the buying process was well facilitated, he will be willing to invest a few shillings for a worthwhile evaluation exercise.

"Thirty days." What's magic about a month? It's a round number, but other than that not, I'm sure what the relevance is. Maybe the right number is ten days, or sixty days, or a year. Based on the business type, this sampling may be too short or long to gain an appropriate measure of success.

"If that goes well, we will talk about plans to go forward." Could Mr. Prospect be more noncommittal? Yet, every day, salespeople say, "Great!" They think that a contract is imminent. Don't underestimate that this could simply be a negotiation ploy by the buying player.

That said, trials and pilots can be incorporated successfully into a buying process where it makes sense. With that in mind, listed below are some of the keys to developing a successful trial or pilot program.

Understand why they want to try versus buy.   This will be different for each prospect and each buying situation. It cannot be assumed that the reason for the trial is known. Even if the salesperson thinks they know, it is more valuable if the prospect articulates his own rationale.

If the trial is successful, develop a concrete next step, i.e., award.
The prospect has asked for something; something should be gained
in return. A question to bring this forward is: If the pilot is successful, what happens next? That next step should be specific with an
associated timeframe. If the prospect can't be specific, a pilot may
not be the best next step.

Develop metrics to measure success. This seems like common
sense, but it is often not formally defined. The provider cannot
perform if it does not know the standard to which it will be measured. The prospect cannot be held accountable for his action step
if there aren't metrics of measurement.

*Formulate a mutually acceptable and beneficial trial period based
on time, volume, etc.* The salesperson should know his business
better than their prospect. At least, I hope this is the case. The
salesperson determines the scope of the trial so he can measure
the desired items. Also, if the pilot is too long, the cost to the
provider may be prohibitive.

Schedule two trial review meetings, midpoint and post-trial.
These meetings are scheduled before the pilot is agreed upon. It's
much more challenging to schedule these when the pilot is under-
way. During these sessions, the performance of the pilot is reviewed
versus the agreed-upon metrics.

*Prepare your company so they deliver consistently with the pre-
scribed metrics.* With the knowledge that a pilot is in place, the
provider's operations leadership can place special attention to the
account so the metrics are achieved.

Own the success of the pilot. If the salesperson doesn't, no one
else will. This means tracking and measuring every step of the
process. For example, have Finance send the invoice to them for
review before sending to the prospect so accuracy is ensured.

"References, Please"

Another completely abused part of the buying process is references. It's interesting. Prospects wouldn't want to be bothered by constant reference calls in support of a provider, but they think nothing of asking for references at any point of the process. A buying process wouldn't be a buying process without the request for client references. Prospects get to a certain step of their selection process and decide they want to speak with three references. I am not sure why three is a magic number, but that seems to be the number that is requested. Rarely are details provided with the request, just the instruction to provide some number of references, usually three.

In most instances, this request triggers a panic e-mail sent to anyone and everyone who can potentially provide recommended client names. Most of the e-mail recipients ignore the request, as they think that someone has already responded to the request. With a little elbow grease, the salesperson eventually formulates a list of some referenceable clients. Typically, it is some combination of the largest and favorite clients. With a few keystrokes in an e-mail, the information is provided to the prospect and the salesperson feels a sigh of relief. "Mission accomplished!" The salesperson sees the finish line, forgetting that many a salesperson has fallen one step short of winning. Yet, this is the traditional approach taken by salespeople in the reference stage of the buying process.

How can references be used strategically in the buying process? To answer this, one first begins with defining the term "reference." According to Webster's Dictionary, the definition of "reference" is someone who can make a statement about a person's qualifications, character, and dependability. Sounds serious! But how many salespeople take that responsibility seriously? How many companies do?

To take this a step further, a reference has value associated with it. It has ownership. A company's referenceable clients are part of its overall *intellectual capital.* Intellectual capital? How can that be? If one were to look at acquisition transactions, one would see that many are done strictly for purchase of the company's client list. It's a key strategic asset, an asset that the company has built and nurtured over many years of investment. It is a key resource often abused by salespeople. As a resource, it needs to be managed and utilized appropriately. With all of this in mind, should a prospect be allowed to determine when it spends a company's intellectual capital? Most of the time, no! However, many salespeople don't give it a second thought. The request is made by the prospect and the list is provided in kind.

But why do prospects ask for references? Most salespeople look at this as a *rubber stamp* in the buying process, allowing the prospect to perform one final due-diligence check before making a provider selection. The always-scary rubber stamp has reappeared! The challenge for the prospect is that providers don't provide the names of unhappy clients. This makes the reference-checking process daunting for prospects. After all, what salespeople are going to provide the name of a client who would give a less-than-stellar reference? The challenge for salespeople is how to gain a competitive advantage in this step of the process. Salespeople are always looking for the one edge that will push them over the top. After all, it is the little things that winning salespeople do that make them winners. So, if all of the competing salespeople are going to provide *good* references, can a salesperson provide the *best* references? Absolutely! But what is the definition of "best?" The answer is that this definition varies from prospect to prospect. It is the job of the salesperson to determine what is "best" on a prospect-by-prospect basis. It is difficult to do if a proper-needs analysis has not been performed.

The best way for a salesperson to develop the list of "best" references is to ask the buying player what is important for him to assess during this exercise. It is a version of a needs analysis. Some of the questions one might ask are:

- How many references would you like?

- What are you hoping to learn from these references?

- How will the reference results affect the final selection decision?

Sometimes getting this kind of information is not possible. This leaves the salesperson to formulate the reference strategy on his own. When selecting references, the salesperson reflects on the process and thinks about what is motivating and driving the buying decision. What are the pain points? What challenges is the prospect having? What are his key criteria when selecting a provider?

One common misconception among salespeople is that the largest client is the best reference. As mentioned earlier, the best reference is prospect-specific. For example, some prospects want to become the provider's largest client; others see that as cause for concern. Whimsically using the largest client in either scenario can create risk to the process. This makes the reference-selection process even more daunting for the salesperson. Obviously, the only reference clients to use are those who are satisfied clients, but the *best* references are the ones who match best with the prospect.

Some of the considerations when selecting a reference:

- Do you have a client whereby the same department or level in the organization made the buying decision?

- Do you have a client who had similar challenges that were resolved when they selected you as their provider?

- Do you have a client who operates in the same industry (SIC code)?

- To measure implementation performance, do you have a new client who can speak to the experience?

- To measure business partnership, do you have a long-term client who can share his experiences and results?

- Do you have a client who came to you from the same competitor as the prospect uses today?

- Do you have a client who is headquartered in the same city or state as the prospect?

- Do you have a client of similar size whether that is in revenue, growth, or employees?

My message is to have a reason why you select particular clients to reference. Whimsically selecting clients for a buying process can give the competition an advantage is they are more thoughtful during the process. With that list determined, a plan is needed, other than finger-crossing, to ensure that this stage of the process further endears the buying player to the provider. The salesperson has an obligation to coach each reference. Not everyone knows how to be a good reference. There isn't training on this subject, and vague answers of "we just love those guys" will not always satisfy the prospect trying to make a selection decision.

But what do clients need to know to provide a stellar reference? What does the salesperson need to do to adequately prepare their client reference?

- Learn who is calling and when, including company name, buying player, and title.

- Discern which products and services the prospect considering buying from you.

- Discover what is important to the prospect in this decision process.

- Ascertain which focal areas you want the client to address with the prospect.

This next point will be the most difficult for a salesperson to implement. If one accepts that a company's clients are its intellectual capital, an invaluable asset, then this next point will make total sense. Ready? Just because a prospect says he wants references, doesn't mean he will get them at that moment. Why? The company needs to control the use of this asset. The salesperson needs to control the process. This means that the company and the salesperson have a say regarding when and how this is used. How often will the same client perform the reference service for a provider? Certainly not every day or every week. In baseball, managers struggle with the right time to insert their pinch hitter because once he is used, he cannot participate in that game again. You can't use the same reference every day. It's all about the strategy.

Consider this dialogue:

"I'm so glad you brought up the point of checking references. We are very passionate about this step of the process and can appreciate the importance of references from your point of view as well. As a matter of fact, we are proud of the database of clients we have who have volunteered to serve as a reference for us.

"However, I have a concern I'd like to share with you.

"We have an understanding with these clients that we will only use them sparingly. We have committed to being sensitive to their time. Typically, what we do is to provide their names when the reference check is the last step of the selection process. In essence, we have been selected and the reference check is the last due diligence.

"Here is where I'm stuck: I value your request and appreciate its importance, but also have a commitment to these clients. What should we do?"

The salesperson has clearly communicated the value of the company's clients and has helped the buying player understand how he will be treated once he is a referenceable client. Most will respect and honor this request. This may also bring about further differentiation, as this is a tangible way in which the provider treats its clients. Those prospects who don't understand should cause the salesperson a moment of pause. What kind of a client is this prospect going to be if he doesn't see the importance of this respect?

A side benefit for the salesperson in utilizing this approach is that the salesperson will know where he stands with this buying player when this part of the process is reached. If the prospect has accepted this condition and is contacting his references, the prospect has selected his provider, pending a successful reference check.

Resolving Client Concerns

There are a variety of descriptions for what I refer to as "resolving client concerns." Some call it overcoming objections, which I find egocentric. They aren't to be overcome, but rather resolved together. Overcoming infers selling. Remember, salespeople facilitate a *buying* process. However, that doesn't mean that preparation is not needed. Far from it! Status quo will come up, and you will need a strategy for that. So will price, and you'll need a strategy for that one, too.

Concerns will arise. Some will be verbalized directly. Others will be inferred based on what has been shared or not shared. There are five types of concerns that will be encountered. Described below are descriptions of those, when they might occur, indicators, and suggestions for resolution.

Concern type: Status Quo

Description: The buying player verbalizes this as a lack of interest in an offering, but it is associated with a failure of the salesperson to excite the prospect to take action.

Phase of buying cycle where this occurs:

- Normally occurs very early in the process, either on the initial call, or within the first meeting.
- Can occur when a new buying player is introduced.
- Can kill the sale if the Wizard has this concern late in the buying process.

Some verbal indicators:

- "We are happy with our current provider."
- "I have another project that has priority. Call me in six months."
- "I have a contract with my current vendor."
- "If it's not broken, why fix it?"
- "We just changed providers and are not prepared to look at this again now."

What the buying player may be communicating:

- I have other priorities more important than this one.
- I don't see the value in the offering.
- I'm afraid of the risks associated with change.
- I don't have the level of influence to drive a change in the organization.

Why the buying player may feel this way:

- Too much on his plate.

- Solution is incongruent with his main objectives.

- Salesperson failed to provide enough motivation to consider a change.

- He fears change.

Keys to resolution:

- Perform research to ensure the proposed solution is congruent with the needs and desires of this buying player as well as the rest of the organization. See the buying player section of the book for more ideas.

- Does the sound-byte demonstrate value to this particular buying player?

- Reaffirm that most clients said the exact the same thing during the initial conversation.

- Cite client examples and why they made the change after further dialogue.

- Review the buying player's profile to identify the best positioning questions for this particular prospect.

- Utilize a few key positioning questions from the needs analysis program that map to this buying player.

- Share with them why you called them in the first place. Many salespeople treat prospects as the call of the day. If this company met the ideal client criteria, share the synergies you see.

- Is this the right buying player with the power to make or heavily influence a change?

Concern type: Price

Description: The price concern occurs for any of a few reasons. The buying player has not seen value demonstrated in the buying process, the salesperson has not differentiated cost versus price, or the prospect is a price buyer only.

Phase of buying cycle where this occurs:

- ◆ Typically occurs at the end of the cycle.
- ◆ Can manifest itself early if buying player requires price to initiate the process.

Some verbal indicators:

- ◆ "All I want to know is, how much?"
- ◆ "You are too expensive."
- ◆ "Your service offers more than we need and it is more expensive that what we have now."
- ◆ "You are priced higher than your competitor."
- ◆ "We only buy through reverse auction."

What buying player may be communicating:

- ◆ He doesn't see the value and only sees commodity.
- ◆ He doesn't see the distinction between price and cost.
- ◆ He may just be negotiating to see the strength of the salesperson's convictions in his price.

Why buying player may feel this way:

- ◆ The salesperson failed to demonstrate value and differentiation.
- ◆ He wants the solution, but wants to see if he can squeeze the price.

Keys to resolution:

- ◆ Take ownership for failing to demonstrate value. Some call this falling on the sword.
- ◆ If this organization only buys based on price, this is best identified early in the needs analysis, so your time was not wasted.

- Ask, "relative to what?" Maybe apples and oranges are being compared.

- "Is the concern cost or price?" If the offering has a strong ROI, help them to focus on the cost versus the price of the solution. The term to master is total cost of ownership. This can help to show the value of the solution. Remember the story of the two cleaning companies shared earlier?

- Reaffirm the areas identified in the needs analysis.

- Differentiation is needed by positioning the full capabilities of the company/offering.

If this is a negotiation ploy, be open and honest, but confident in your conviction that the price provided is consistent with the value shared. Procurement agents regularly tell providers that their price is too high. This is their job, to negotiate the best possible price. Don't flinch! Feel confident in the pricing you put forward. If not, margin and commissions are sacrificed.

- Is this the right prospect to pursue? Hopefully, this company meets the ideal client criteria and they are the right prospect to pursue. If not, you own this issue. It's a painful lesson learned.

Concern type: Trust

Description: This concern comes about due to poor historical experiences with your company, poor experiences with the current provider, or doubts about presented benefits.

Phase of buying cycle where this occurs:

- This can appear at any point of the process.

Some verbal indicators:

- "We used you in the past and weren't satisfied with your service."

- "You *all* say you have the best people, service, and technology."

- "We want to do a pilot before moving ahead with the full solution."

What the buying player may be communicating:

- Fear, uncertainty, and doubt
- Adverse to taking risks

Why buying player may feel this way:

- Bad experiences
- Fear of accountability

Keys to resolution:

- Ask questions to ensure a complete understanding of the concern and why it exists. Don't try to guess why they feel this way, try to have them share it.

- Ask the client what will help him to move past the concern. After all, it's his concern. Only he knows what it will take for him to feel comfortable.

- If the prospect had a bad experience with your firm in the past, share with them what has changed.

- Don't try to sell. This is not to be overcome, but to be worked through. Trust cannot be fixed by your overcoming it.

- Provide proof documentation when appropriate.

- For pilots, what is going to be measured? What does success look like? How will account management be measured? See the section on pilots for more ideas.

Concern type: Shortcomings

Description: These are concerns whereby the prospect has a specific requirement that the provider cannot provide.

Phase of buying cycle where this occurs:

◆ This becomes apparent during needs analysis.

Some verbal indicators:

◆ "We only want a blue gadget."

◆ "It must include all of these things."

◆ "Speed is critical."

What buying player may be communicating:

◆ He has formulated his own criteria for the solution.

◆ Another buying player has specific criteria that he requires.

Why the buying player may feel this way:

◆ His current provider offers this.

◆ A competitor provides this.

◆ He created the scope based on his experiences and pain.

Keys to resolution:

◆ Make sure the requirement is completely understood.

◆ If it is, how critical is that element, to whom, and why?

◆ Does this solution include things that are also important to that buying player which he cannot get elsewhere?

◆ Use of effective positioning questions is the key to resolution.

◆ Check with management to make sure this requirement cannot be satisfied.

◆ Should this prospect have been pursued in the first place if this is a major consideration of his?

◆ If this cannot be resolved, get out quick! No point in trying to become a hero. If the solution is not a match for the prospect's needs, move on to someone who *does* match.

Concern type: Buying Player Authority

Description: This concern occurs when the buying player does not appear to have the authority to act.

Phase of buying cycle where this occurs:

- Can occur at anytime, but is most likely to occur early.

Some verbal indicators:

- "We are decentralized and I have no control over what the field does."

- "We can't get any time from IT to discuss possible improvements."

- "We can't dictate to the field."

- "I like your service, but my boss prefers someone else."

- "I have to meet with my boss to discuss any changes we would consider."

- "We only buy through RFPs."

- "This must go to a committee for decision."

What the buying player may be communicating:

- Not a priority to him.

- He is not authorized to pursue new solutions.

Why the buying player may feel this way:

- Other parts of his job are more important.

- The problems are not that painful.

- His rank is not high enough in his organization to drive a change.

Keys to resolution:

- Request an introduction to higher-level players.

- ◆ Become an advocate to help this buying player get what he desires for his specific reasons.

- ◆ Qualify buying players early in the process.

With a plan to resolve each of the five concerns, preparation is complete. The recipe for success has been written. Nevertheless, some deals will be lost. To quote one of my favorites, Dr. Seuss:

> **"And will you succeed? Yes! You will, indeed! (98 and 3/4 percent guaranteed)"**

The Deal Autopsy

Continuing with Dr. Seuss,

> "Except when you don't.
> Because sometimes, you won't.
> I'm sorry to say so
> But, sadly it's true
> That Bang-ups
> And Hang-ups
> Can happen to you."

Winning is fun and it's contagious. I'm sure someone has told you that as long as you did your best, you should be happy. Baloney! If you are in sales, and you did your best and you lost, what did you make in commissions? Answer: *zero*. I agree in always striving to do your best, but no one has a 100-percent win percentage. Not in any sport, certainly, not in sales.

When you don't win (or dare I say, lose), what you learn from the experience will help you to win next time. In essence, an autopsy is required to be performed on the buying process to understand why the deal died. I assure you that this is a painful exercise. You won't enjoy it at all, but if you are honest with yourself, it is adds another invaluable tool to your kit.

1. How was this prospect identified?

2. What buying players were met?

3. Who were you unable to meet?

4. Who was the Mentor?

5. What was his strength ranking?

6. What was his influence ranking?

7. Who was the Saboteur?

8. What was the strategy to diffuse the Saboteur?

9. What reason was given as to why the prospect did not select this solution?

10. Did the prospect select another provider, or did status quo win?

11. If the process were to begin today, what was learned that would allow for a different strategy to be utilized?

CHAPTER 12
Parting Thoughts

"Keep your dreams alive. Understand to achieve anything requires faith and belief in yourself, vision, hard work, determination, and dedication. Remember all things are possible for those who believe."

—Gail Devers

Muscle Memory

In the gym, muscle memory is the feeling the body experiences when doing a particular exercise. As one continues with an exercise program, his body goes on autopilot. He is no longer thinking about how to perform each exercise. His body has a memory system, which executes based on repetition. His body knows that in a certain situation, it is to perform certain movements.

The first time someone exercises, the feeling is uncomfortable. The movements are not ones that are commonly performed by non-fitness enthusiasts. Some people allow the discomfort to dominate their mind and they give up exercising all together. Others commit to exercise, as they have certain goals that they desire to achieve. While they were initially uncomfortable, they committed to feeling comfortable "feeling uncomfortable." These are the people who succeed.

I recognize that many of the philosophies and approaches in this book are new. It certainly requires the commitment of time to implement them successfully. Rest assured, it will be uncomfortable for a while. That is to be expected. Transitioning the approach from one whereby prospects are sold to, to an approach whereby a buying process is facilitated, will not happen overnight. However, commitment to change is an important first step and will help to ensure success.

The process is best illustrated by the story between a borderline professional golfer and his trainer (golf pro). The golfer recognized that he had to improve his putting if he were going to take his career to the next level. He went to his golf pro for help. After watching some practice shots, the golf pro gave the following advice, "Move your thumb here. Turn your hand like this. Angle your right arm like that. Tilt your hips forward. Straighten your back. Move this foot over here. Turn your knee like this."

Having turned himself into a pretzel, the golfer told his pro that he was uncomfortable. The pro responded, "That's true. It is uncomfortable. However, you have choices. You can keep putting the way you were and never make the pro circuit. Or you can feel comfortable "feeling uncomfortable" and take your game to the next level. The choice is yours."

Potential Pitfalls

Having committed to change, you should be aware that there are some common pitfalls that can sneak in and destroy the process. Watch out for these.

Selling versus facilitating the buying process. Just remember the quote from Gitomer and you will never go wrong. "People don't like to be sold-but they love to buy."

Pursuing everyone. Focusing on a very specific profile that is geared toward the ideal prospect creates wealthy salespeople. Most salespeople are successful by effectively selling a few prospects an entire solution versus pursuit of the masses.

Focusing on "better" instead of "different." Unless there is irrefutable proof of "better" in a context that matters to a buyer, don't bother to use it. Be different instead. It's much more powerful.

Unique, but can't communicate it effectively. The investment needed to develop an effective sound-byte is minimal when compared to how critical that component becomes in the buying process. If the difference can't be clearly articulated, no one will ever know about it.

Failing to address status quo before the other competitors. Recalling that two types of competitors are encountered, each is defeated in a different manner.

Oops, that's not a Mentor. Just because a buying player likes you, doesn't mean they meet the criteria of a Mentor.

One is the loneliest number. Falling in love with the nicest buying player and not expanding the influence in the organization can jeopardize the sale.

Failing to use buying player language. Speak his language to build the relationship.

Follow the Boy Scout motto and "Be Prepared!" Much of what has been shared requires you to learn your business and your clientele. Invest in yourself, so you effectively facilitate the buying process.

Aye, Aye!!! This pitfall refers to constantly speaking in the first person. Think of the pirate asking their prisoner to walk the plank. It's not about you; it's about the buying players.

School is in session. Successful selling is not about the demonstration to a client of a salesperson's vast knowledge. The old proverb of being an *interested* person instead of an *interesting* person applies.

Feeling the draft. Forgetting to use insulators at key points of the process can create a cold response from prospects.

@$% happens. Plan for when things don't go exactly as planned. Learn from the experience so you improve your game.

The following is the diatribe of a fallen sales hero:

Sorry, Can't Sell Today
by Willie McMoney

Can't sell in January . . . Between the terrible weather and everyone coming back from vacation, how can you expect someone to focus on buying now? I'll pound the pavement next month.

Can't sell in February . . . More snow and more vacation. Way to go, Washington and Lincoln; thanks for President's Day! It's such a short month. No one can make a decision in such a short month. Next month is going to be better.

Can't sell in March . . . No one is going to make a decision on this with more holidays around the corner. Good time to shop for summer clothes. I'll just borrow money because I'll make huge commissions later to pay it back.

Can't sell in April . . . Who wants to focus on buying with spring in the air? And hey, my kid's birthday is this month. I'm sure my prospects are working on their taxes anway. Next month will be better for sure.

Can't sell in May . . . Great weather in May, and I hear that my prospect may be thinking about being acquired. No problem. I'll look for better ones next month. There's tons of opportunity out there.

Can't sell in June . . . Kids are getting out of school. Wow! I almost forgot Flag Day. No one buys in this weather. Besides, July is a better month for sales anyway.

Can't sell in July . . .   Great time of year to be at the beach and enjoying the outdoors. I think all of my contacts are on vacation... together! Nope, can't sell this month.

Can't sell in August . . .   Too hot! Besides, I'm taking my vacation. They Probably are too. No selling to be done now. Next month, for sure.

Can't sell in September . . .   Between the three-day Labor Day weekend and a new fiscal year kicking in, no one is buying anything. I'm feeling good about next month.

Can't sell in October . . .   Columbus' birthday; what should I get him this year? I almost forgot Halloween! I'm going to focus on selling hard over the next two months. I'll finish the year strong.

Can't sell in November . . .   Thanksgiving, ya know. Very short month. I don't think any of my contacts have their budget yet. Can't buy without a budget. Man, December is going to rock!

Can't sell in December . . .   Everyone is on vacation in December. I know I am! Who can focus on buying with the end of the year so close? What should I do for Festivus this year?

Oh well, maybe next year will be better for sales. Luckily, no one is buying anything from anyone this year.

Index

WIN WEALTH WORTH WITH WBUSINESS BOOKS

Sales

First 100 Days of Selling: A Practical Day-by-Day Guide to Excel in the Sales Profession
ISBN 13: 978-0-8329-5004-9

By Jim Ryerson

Price: $22.95 USD

Great Salespeople Aren't Born, They're Hired: The Secrets to Hiring Top Sales Professionals
ISBN 13: 978-0-8329-5000-1

By Joe Miller

Price: $19.95 USD

Hire, Fire, & the Walking Dead: A Leaders Guide to Recruiting the Best
ISBN 13: 978-0-8329-5001-8

By Greg Moran with Patrick Longo
Price: $19.95 USD

Marketing

What's Your BQ? Learn How 35 Companies Add Customers, Subtract Competitors, and Multiply Profits with Brand Quotient
ISBN 13: 978-0-8329-5002-5

By Sandra Sellani

Price: $24.95 USD

Reality Sells: How to Bring Customers Back Again and Again by Marketing Your Genuine Story
ISBN 13: 978-0-8329-5008-7

By Bill Guertin and Andrew Corbus

Price: $19.95 USD

Entrepreneurship

The N Factor: How Efficient Networking Can Change the Dynamics of Your Business
ISBN 13: 978-0-8329-5006-3

By Adrie Reinders and Marion Freijsen
Price: $19.95 USD

Thriving Latina Entrepreneurs in America
ISBN 13: 978-0-8329-5007-0

By Maria de Lourdes Sobrino
Price: $24.95 USD

Millionaire by 28
ISBN 13: 978-0-8329-5010-0

By Todd Babbitt
Price: $19.95 USD

Check out these books at your local bookstore or at
www.Wbusinessbooks.com

THIS BOOK DOESN'T END
AT THE LAST PAGE

Log on to **www.WBusiness.biz** and join the WBusiness community.

Share your thoughts, talk to the author, and learn from other community members in the forums. **www.WBusiness.biz** is a place you can sharpen your skills, learn the new trends and network with other sales professionals.